Stories
of Popular Hymns

BY
Kathleen Blanchard

FOURTH EDITION

ZONDERVAN PUBLISHING HOUSE
Grand Rapids, Michigan

EIGHT FORTY-SEVEN OTTAWA AVENUE, N.W.
GRAND RAPIDS, MICHIGAN

STORIES OF
POPULAR HYMNS

A FOREWORD

It AFFORDS me great pleasure to write a foreword for this little book and that for several reasons. First of all, it is so on account of my life long association and friendship with the Blanchard family, Dr. R. J. Blanchard having been for long years my skilful and highly esteemed family physician. Secondly, because of my warm approval of the contents of the volume which I have read with great care and appreciation. The volume gives ample evidence of the wide reading and painstaking research on the part of the authoress and as a result she has done her work most ably and admirably. Thirdly, I have learned to value highly any revealing of the circumstances surrounding the composition of a hymn and the impulse which moved and possessed the author at the time. I realized this when after my retirement a few years ago I found myself able to read widely, a privilege which the duties of my office had hitherto precluded. In reading Biographies I was greatly impressed with the added personal interest in some of our familiar hymns which was produced by the disclosure of the conditions prevailing in the author's life when he composed it. Did space permit I could give many instances of this. For example; when, in perusing the biography of the author, I had a glimpse into the sacred precincts of his home life and discovered that the words of the hymn owed the impulse which inspired them to an incident, a joy or a sorrow, in the family life, they possessed ever afterward a new meaning for me and touched something in me that they had never done before. Previously the amazing intellect of the author may have captured my imagination, afterwards his heart spoke to my heart and made his words live forever as a dominating force in my life. In a similar way Mrs. Blanchard's record of the conditions and circumstances connected with the composition and publication of the different hymns will, I trust, prove of great value and for that reason I heartily commend her work to those who will have the privilege of reading it.

S. P. MATHESON, *Archbishop and formerly Primate of the Anglican Church of all Canada*

PREFACE

THE AUTHOR is gratefully indebted to many sources for the information contained in this small work. It is not the product of original research; but merely an attempt to put into popular form material and anecdotes on a subject dear to many people. The little book will have achieved its purpose if it supplies a background for some familiar hymns for those who constantly sing them.

K. B.

· I N D E X ·

Index

INTRODUCTION

POETRY HAS always had a charm for human thought. It was the earliest form of literary appeal. Because of its rhythm and its imagery it becomes the earliest medium of education. In some spheres of thought it still remains such. Hymns are a persistent type of poetical literature and have found expression outside the area of Christian religion.

Because Christianity is a form of religion based on the noblest emotions of the human soul, hymns have found there a distinctly congenial soil. Faith, love, gratitude, hope combined with pity, compassion and unselfish sacrifices are the characteristic feelings of life as it is quickened and sustained by Christian devotion and these have been fruitful in producing the noblest hymns of all time. Hymns, therefore, have come to form a striking part of our literary inheritance and are perhaps more widely used and more generally appreciate than any other form of poetical expression Thousands and tens of thousands of voices use them twice every Sunday throughout the wide expanse of Christian worship and yet little attention is given to them in our multiplied areas of literary interpretation.

Much interest would be added to the widespread use of this literature if people fully understood the elements which combine to give hymns their popular appeal; much could be added by creating a keen sensitivity to the imagery in the hymns, and by cultivating a fine appreciation of the delightful delicacy of expression and suggestion of the arresting force manifest in the selection of words, and in the use of attractive phrases. These coupled with a knowledge of the writers and the circumstances which lead to the production must prove a helpful incentive to the thoughtful use of hymns.

Mrs. Kathleen Blanchard has placed the public under a very heavy obligation by supplying for a great bulk of our hymns these last two essential factors. She has done this in a simple easy style. The facts are stated in clear straightforward language and in expression well within the compass of the general range of thought. I have read with keen delight many of her stories in the *Free Press* and now welcome the prospect of seeing these in book form. This book as it satisfies a conscious need in the public mind, must therefore meet a very heavy public response.

J. H. RIDDELL, D.D., *Retired president of United College, Winnipeg, Manitoba, Canada.*

Stories of Popular Hymns

"ABIDE WITH ME"

OF ALL the hymns that have been written there is
none more universally loved or better known than
"Abide with Me."

The Rev. Francis Lyte was born at Kelso, Ireland,
in 1793. His father, Captain Lyte, died while he was
still a child, so he went with his mother to live in
Dublin and was educated there. He wished to study
medicine, but the church called him and he took Holy
Orders at the early age of twenty-two. He then had
a curacy at Wexford, Ireland. After two years he
moved to Cornwall, England, and while there he went
through a spiritual change, which shaped and in-
fluenced his future life. It was through the illness
and death of a brother clergyman, which greatly af-
fected him.

In 1819 he went to Lymington, where he worked for
four years, and in doing so, overtaxed his strength,
and began to show signs of tuberculosis. He was offered and accepted the fisherman's parish of Brixham-
on-Sea, where he hoped to regain his health. Brixham
seaport in Devonshire is well known in history. William
of Orange first landed there in 1688. One of the
treasures shown to visitors is the stone onto which

he stepped. Nearly a century and a half later
William IV trod on the same stone when he came
to Brixham on a less historic mission and was delighted to be met by Mr. Lyte with a surpliced
choir. Mr. Lyte was already known through the
hymns he had written. Two of them are: "Pleasant
Are Thy Courts Above," "Praise My Soul the King
of Heaven."

Francis Lyte felt very much the sadness and tender-
ness of life. It was a strange chance that placed so
sensitive and frail a minister with fisher-folk. Suffering from tuberculosis, he felt that his time on earth
was short and he wanted to do something for his people.

William IV stayed sometimes at Berryhead House,
Brixham. He died there in 1837 and gave this beautiful home to Mr. Lyte—a gift in return for kindness.
Here Mr. Lyte lived for ten years, happy in his home
and parish.

In the late summer of 1847 his doctors informed him
that he must give up all work and spend the winters
in the south of France, for his strength was slowly
ebbing away. Arrangements were quickly made. The
last Sunday came for service with his people. In moving language he said farewell. There was scarcely a
dry eye in the church as the simple fisher-folk watched
him go down the aisle for the last time. It was a beautiful September day. He wandered into the garden
and sat down on a bank overlooking Torbay, the sea
at his feet, the gentle rustle of the leaves overhead,
the sky a canopy of beauty, the clouds of night in the
distance. Who can say what his thoughts were? He
asked to leave something to help humanity. Even as

he mused, his wish was answered. He went indoors and in anguish of parting from all he loved, he wrote—

Abide with me; fast falls the eventide;
The darkness deepens, Lord, with me abide;
When other helpers fail, and comforts flee,
Help of the helpless, O abide with me.

Swift to its close ebbs out life's little day:
Earth's joys grow dim, its glories pass away:
Change and decay in all around I see;
O Thou, who changest not, abide with me.

He gave this to his adopted daughter that night. The next morning he left for France and died there less than three months after leaving Brixham. He is buried in a flower-filled cemetery at Nice, but the hymn he wrote on his last Sunday at home will never die as long as the English language is sung.

:-:-:-:

"ALL GLORY, LAUD, AND HONOR"

St. Theodulph of Orleans was born in Italy about the year 770. As a young man he entered a monastery. His learning, diplomacy, and skill marked him for advancement, and in due course he was chosen abbot.

During the stormy days of those turbulent times, soldiers ruled the streets, brawls were common, and fighting was an everyday event. The Abbot Theodulph was sought as a mediator of the different factions. He came to the notice of the great soldier, Charlemagne, who thought highly of his ability—so much so that when the Emperor returned to France he took Theodulph with him, and he was made Bishop of Orleans.

This appointment, and Charlemagne's favor, brought him many enemies who conspired to encompass his ruin. Courtiers whispered tales into King Louis' ear, suspicion was aroused, and Theodulph was arrested and imprisoned in a monastery at Angers, where he languished for three long years, closely confined.

While so imprisoned he may have composed a long poem of the Mediæval church to be used for the great procession of the people on the Sunday before Easter. On Palm Sunday of the year 821 A.D., King Louis and his retinue were on their way to church. Passing the prison they heard joyful strains and reined in their steeds to listen. It was Theodulph, singing through the bars of his window the hymn he had composed for that day. The King's heart was softened by such fervor, and turning to his knights, he declared, "This bishop is no traitor!" He ordered his release at once and restored him to his see and royal favor.

The good Theodulph died soon afterwards. His inspired spirit left to posterity this eloquent hymn of praise for Palm Sunday. It has come down from age to age, over eleven hundred years. In 1854 the great translator, Dr. Neale, gave us this from the Latin. It was soon to be found in all the hymn books.

> *All glory, laud, and honor*
> *To Thee, Redeemer, King,*
> *To Whom the lips of children*
> *Made sweet hosannas ring!*
>
> *Thou art the King of Israel,*
> *Thou David's royal Son,*
> *Who in the Lord's name comest,*
> *The King and Blessed One.*

All glory . . . .
The company of angels
Are praising Thee on high,
And mortal men and all things
Created make reply.

All glory . . . .
The people of the Hebrews
With palms before Thee went;
Our praise and prayer and anthems
Before Thee we present.

All glory . . . .
To Thee before Thy passion
They sang their hymns of praise;
To Thee now high exalted
Our melody we raise.

All glory . . . .
Thou didst accept their praises;
Accept the prayers we bring,
Who in all good delightest,
Thou good and gracious King.

:-:-:-:

"ALL HAIL THE POWER OF JESUS' NAME!"

THIS MAJESTIC hymn, written in 1779, came out first in the *Gospel Magazine* of the following year. The author was Edward Perronet, born at Shoreham, Kent, 1721, the son of the local vicar.

Charles Wesley and Edward Perronet were friends and contemporaries. In Charles Wesley's diary of 1775 he mentioned Edward, in the vexed question of separation from the Anglican Churches, to which the Wesleys were strongly opposed and Edward Perronet's family favored. It is reported that the Wesleys refused the admission of this hymn into their collection, but there is a remarkable story told of how this hymn eventually became a great power.

About one hundred years ago a Methodist local preacher named "Billy" Dawson was preaching in London on the divinity of Christ. Dawson was a very amazing character. He was a Yorkshire farmer, but his vivid imagination and personal magnetism enabled him to sway large audiences. On this occasion he was speaking at a vast meeting; during his talk he portrayed the Savior as teacher and priest. He began to paint a word picture—His glory as a King in His own right over saints and angels. With eloquent warmth at the thought, he depicted a coronation pageant. The great procession, with prophets and patriarchs, apostles and martyrs, moved forward. The massive temple was filled with the great and noble array. At the climax of the thought, the preacher suddenly broke from his ordinary tone and shouted—

All hail the power of Jesus' name,
Let angels prostrate fall;
Bring forth the royal diadem
And crown Him Lord of all.

Crown Him, ye martyrs of your God,
Who from His altar call;
Extol the stem of Jesse's Rod
And crown Him Lord of all.

Ye seed of Israel's chosen race,
Ye ransomed from the fall,
Hail Him Who saves you by His grace,
And crown Him Lord of all.

Hail Him, ye heirs of David's line
Whom David Lord did call,
The God Incarnate, Man Divine,
And crown Him Lord of all.

Sinners, whose love can ne'er forget
The wormwood and the gall,
Go spread your trophies at His feet
And crown Him Lord of all.

Let every tribe and every tongue
Before Him prostrate fall,
Join in the universal song
And crown Him Lord of all.

The scene was overwhelming. The crowd sprang to their feet and sang this hymn with a feeling and a power that seemed to swell higher and higher at every verse— such was the wonderful result of Edward Perronet's verses.

About 1800 William Shrubsole wrote the tune "Miles Lane" while at Canterbury Cathedral, and this setting is generally used in England. The tune called "Coronation" is mostly used on the American Continent; it was composed by Oliver Holden, a carpenter.

"ASLEEP IN JESUS"

MRS. MARGARET MACKAY, a native of Inverness, Scotland, had been visiting friends in different parts of England and was now staying at a little village in Devonshire. It was spring — and one sunny morning rambling down the unfamiliar lanes she came upon a path leading to a village church. Letting the

latch in the wicket-gate, she went into the churchyard,
pausing to admire the beauty before her—the silent
mounds carpeted with primroses.

She sat on the grass listening to the song of the birds
in the trees, while a sense of peace and rest surrounded
her, unlike anything she had ever felt before. Rising,
she wandered down the neatly kept path, and her attention was attracted by an inscription on an ancient
stone, "Sleeping in Jesus."

On reaching home with the haunting words repeating
themselves in her mind, she was inspired to write this
hymn:

> *Asleep in Jesus, blessed sleep,*
> *From which none ever wakes to weep!*
> *A calm and undisturbed repose,*
> *Unbroken by the last of foes.*
>
> *Asleep in Jesus! O how sweet*
> *To be for such a slumber meet!*
> *With holy confidence to sing*
> *That Death hath lost his venomed sting.*
>
> *Asleep is Jesus! peaceful rest,*
> *Whose waking is supremely blest!*
> *No fear, no woe, shall dim that hour*
> *That manifests the Savior's power.*
>
> *Asleep in Jesus! O for me*
> *May such a blissful refuge be!*
> *Securely shall my ashes lie,*
> *Waiting the summons from on high.*
>
> *Asleep in Jesus! far from thee*
> *Thy kindred and their graves may be,*
> *But thine is still a blessed sleep*
> *From which none ever wakes to weep.*

Mrs. MacKay died at Cheltenham at the age of seventy-
six. There is no record that she wrote any other hymn.

"ART THOU WEARY, ART THOU LANGUID?"

In Palestine there is a monastery built high up on a bald peak of rock, with sheer cliff down one side. This fortress-like place is the famous retreat of Mar Saba. It is situated in a very dreary part of the rocky scrub of the Kedron Valley, half way between Jerusalem and the Dead Sea, and is almost inaccessible to the outside world. For centuries cells have been built by the monks among the rocks. In each generation some famous men have here sought peace and solitude. The world has been enriched by manuscripts recorded down the ages from this most desolate abode.

In the year 780, there was a monk living there by the name of Stephen (known afterwards as St. Stephen). He was the nephew of the famous St. John of Damascus (the hymn-writer).

Through the centuries, the Mar Saba monastery has suffered attack, sometimes by bedouin Arabs, often by Moslems and Persians. Each powerful race has in turn tried to gain this rocky fastness, but nothing has dislodged the Order—and today, Mar Saba is still inhabited.

The records show that about the year 780 A. D., Stephen, taking the verse from the original Greek Testament, "Come unto Me all ye that labor and are heavy laden, and I will give you rest," wrote this hymn in the form of question and answer.

The manuscripts were preserved with the greatest care. Then in 1862, Dr. Neale, the distinguished translator, gave this now famous hymn to the world. It was published in *Hymns Ancient and Modern* to the tune "Stephanos," harmonized by W. H. Monk.

Art thou weary, art thou languid,
Art thou sore distrest?
"Come to Me" saith One, "and coming
Be at rest!"

Hath He marks to lead me to Him,
If He be my Guide?
"In His feet and hands are wound prints,
And His side."

Is there diadem as Monarch
That His brow adorns?
"Yea, a crown, in very surety
But of thorns."

If I find Him, if I follow,
What His guerdon here?
"Many a sorrow, many a labor
Many a tear."

If I still hold closely to Him,
What hath He at last?
"Sorrow vanquished, labor ended,
Jordan past."

If I ask Him to receive me,
Will He say me nay?
"Not till earth, and not till heav'n
Pass away."

:-:-:-:

"AT EVEN, ERE THE SUN WAS SET"

In 1868, *Hymns Ancient and Modern* was in the hands of the board of revisers (of which Sir Henry Baker was the guiding force). The need was felt for more evening hymns for the new edition.

On writing to his friend, Canon Twells, Sir Henry

confided this fact and asked him if he could send along something suitable.

Canon Twells was well known in the scholastic world. He was headmaster of the famous Godolphin Grammar school, Hammersmith, London. His time was greatly occupied, and he found few occasions for quiet thought. However, the day at last came when one late afternoon the canon had to stay quietly in the schoolroom while the boys were writing their examination papers.

He relates how he sat thinking of the request for a hymn. Just at that time the sun had reached the stage where it sent a beautiful glow through some colored windows near by. It was getting towards evening, and his mind became absorbed in the appealing account in Mark 1:32: "At even, when the sun did set, they brought unto Him all that were diseased, and them that were possessed with devils. And all the city was gathered together at the door."

The canon's mood was a receptive one. His sensitive mind was at once drawn to portray in words the beautiful scene his imagination conjured. With pen and paper before him, he wrote each verse as though inspired. As the boys finished their work, so did Canon Twells complete the hymn.

> At even, ere the sun was set,
>   The sick, O Lord, around Thee lay:
> Oh, in what divers pains they met!
>   Oh, with what joy they went away.
>
> Once more 'tis eventide, and we
>   Oppressed with various ills draw near:
> What if Thy form we cannot see?
>   We know and feel that Thou art here.

O Savior Christ, our woes dispel:
For some are sick, and some are sad,
And some have never loved Thee well,
And some have lost the love they had;

And some have found the world is vain,
Yet from the world they break not free;
And some have friends who give them pain,
Yet have not sought a friend in Thee:

And none, O Lord, have perfect rest,
For none are wholly free from sin;
And they, who fain would serve Thee best,
Are conscious most of wrong within.

Thy touch has still its ancient power!
No word from Thee can fruitless fall;
Hear, in this solemn evening hour,
And in Thy mercy heal us all.

This hymn has been translated into many languages. The author left on record his thanks to God for allowing him to be of some service in bringing souls to the knowledge of His kingdom.

The melody was taken from an early German source and specially adapted for use in *Hymns Ancient and Modern*.

"BE PRESENT AT OUR TABLE, LORD"

IN THE YEAR 1718 there lived in London, England, a Quaker family named Cennick, an immigrant from Bohemia who had changed his name to English spelling. A son, John, was born to them that year, who, as he grew up, showed signs of literary talent. When a young man he became a land surveyor. He lived at Reading where he became acquainted with the Wesleys.

John Wesley asked young Cennick to go to Kingswood, a mining town, to teach the colliers' children. So he became the first Methodist lay preacher.

After some years at this work, he parted from the Wesleys as a result of a disagreement. He came under the influence of Whitefield, but his whole heart turned to the Moravians. He joined their brotherhood, working for them both in Germany and North Ireland.

When Cennick was a young man of twenty-three, he wrote this short poem, unequalled in beauty and known the world over:

> Be present at our table, Lord,
> Be here, and everywhere adored;
> Thy creatures bless, and grant that we
> May feast in paradise with Thee.

In 1741 it was brought out in a book called *Cennick's Sacred Hymns for Children of God in the Days of Their Pilgrimage.*

:-:-:-:

"BLEST BE THE TIE THAT BINDS"

In 1772, the Rev. John Fawcett was the Baptist minister of a poor country parish at Wainsgate, Yorkshire. The salary he received was so meagre that his family scarcely had enough to support life. As the children grew older, the need for taking some steps to improve his financial position became imperative.

At last an opportunity was presented. Mr. Fawcett

was offered and accepted a call to a church in London, with a substantial stipend. The day came for his last sermon. The next day the wagons arrived to load the family goods for the new home.

When the village folk saw the furniture being moved, their sorrow knew no bounds. The house was soon surrounded by weeping people, who begged their beloved pastor not to leave them. Mrs. Fawcett was so overcome by this display of grief that she called to her husband, "O John, John, we cannot go!" "No," said the good man, "I cannot go, either; we will stay here!" And at once he gave orders for all the things to be unloaded and taken back into the house.

His resolve was received with the greatest joy. The story goes that the talented Dr. John Fawcett remained in the country parish "poor but rich" on $125 a year and the love and attachment of his people. He wrote the following for them to celebrate the event:

Blest be the tie that binds
Our hearts in Christian love;
The fellowship of kindred minds
Is like to that above.

Before our Father's throne
We pour our ardent prayers:
Our fears, our hopes, our aims are one:
Our comforts and our cares.

We share each other's woes,
Each other's burdens bear:
And often for each other flows
The sympathizing tear.

When for a while we part
This thought will soothe our pain:
That we shall still be joined in heart,
And one day meet again.

One glorious hope revives
Our courage by the way:
While each in expectation lives,
And longs to see the day.

When from all toil and pain
And sin we shall be free
And perfect love and friendship reign
Through all eternity.

It became the pleasant custom for the singers of this hymn to join hands as a symbol of friendship. It is a favorite at church meetings. The tune generally used (Bethlehem) was composed by Samuel Wesley and was used in 1837—in "Service of the Church."

:-:-:-:

"BREATHE ON ME, BREATH OF GOD"

EDWIN HATCH, D.D., was born in Derby, England. He was educated at King Edward School, Birmingham, and Pembroke College, Oxford. His friends and contemporaries at Oxford included Burne Jones, William Morris, and Swinburne—all of them destined to find fame in the arts.

Hatch was brought up a nonconformist but early in life he adopted the Anglican faith and was ordained. He worked in a slum parish in the East End of London, but in 1859 accepted the Chair of Classics at Trinity College, Quebec. After some years there, he became Rector of Quebec High School, spending eight years altogether in Canada.

He was then invited to become vice-principal of

St. Mary's Hall, Oxford, England. It was during this
time that he wrote the wonderful prayer-hymn:

> *Breathe on me, Breath of God,*
> *Fill me with life anew,*
> *That I may love what Thou dost love,*
> *And do what Thou would'st do.*
>
> *Breathe on me, Breath of God,*
> *Until my heart is pure:*
> *Until my will is one with Thine*
> *To do and to endure.*
>
> *Breathe on me, Breath of God,*
> *Till I am wholly Thine:*
> *Until this earthly part of me*
> *Glows with Thy fire divine.*
>
> *Breathe on me, Breath of God,*
> *So shall I never die,*
> *But live with Thee the perfect life*
> *Of Thine eternity.*

Of profound learning, Edwin Hatch was an acknowledged master in the scholastic world. His noble character combined with great understanding and simplicity
of nature left its stamp on his work which nothing
could efface. Loved by his confreres and held in reverence by his pupils, he died at the early age of fifty-
three, and was mourned by all.

"CHRISTIANS, AWAKE!"

"WHAT WOULD you like for Christmas, Dolly?" John
Byrom asked his little daughter over two hundred years
ago!

"Oh, something I can always keep," said she.
"Very well, we will see what can be done about it,"
replied her father. "I will write you a carol."
On Christmas morning, when Dolly came down to
breakfast, he presented her with an ordinary sheet of
paper, neatly folded, and written on it, "Christmas
Day for Dolly."
It was:

> Christians, awake, salute this happy morn,
> Whereon the Savior of mankind is born.
> Rise to adore the mystery of love,
> Which hosts of angels chanted from above:
> > With them the joyful tidings first begun
> > Of God Incarnate, and a Virgin's Son.
>
> Then to the watchful shepherds it was told,
> Who heard the angelic herald's voice, "Behold,
> I bring you tidings of a Savior's birth
> To you and all the nations upon earth:
> > This day hath God fulfilled His promised word;
> > This day is born a Savior, Christ the Lord."
>
> He spake: and straight the celestial choir
> In hymns of joy, unknown before conspire:
> The praises of redeeming love they sang,
> And Heaven's whole orb with alleluias rang:
> > God's highest glory was their anthem still,
> > "Peace upon earth and unto men good-will."
>
> O may we keep and ponder in our mind
> God's wondrous love in saving lost mankind:
> Trace we the Babe, who has retrieved our loss,
> From His poor manger to His bitter cross:
> > Tread in His steps, assisted by His grace,
> > Till man's first heavenly state again takes place.

Little did the family think that their father that
day had written a carol that would last for generations
yet unborn.

The manuscript was shown round to their friends by Dolly, and by great good fortune John Wainwright, who was the organist of Manchester Old Parish Church, saw it and set it to the well known tune. He had a surprise in store for the author, as the next Christmas Eve, Wainwright took his choristers over to Byrom's home, and John and his family stood round the porch thrilled as they listened for the first time to the carol now so well known.

The manuscript is carefully kept, also Byrom's portrait, in the Chetham Library, Manchester, his birthplace. John Byrom is buried in Manchester Cathedral, and John Wainwright lies at Stockport, near by.

In John Byrom's note book there is an entry, "Christmas, 1750. The singing men and boys with Mr. Wainwright came here and sang, 'Christians Awake.'"

The tune is regarded as being first sung in Stockport Parish Church on the day this entry was made. It was not published for a number of years but was in *Ashcroft's Collections*, 1760.

:-:-:-:

"COME, HOLY GHOST, OUR SOULS INSPIRE"
Veni Creator Spiritus

THIS GREAT Latin hymn was the *Te Deum* of the middle ages. Some historians have traced its origin to the ninth century. The author is unknown, but it belonged to the Medieval Church.

A French Chronicler, Joinville, illustrates how much this hymn was in use in the year of our Lord 1248, with the following story:

A fleet of ships was waiting to sail at Roche-de-Marseille. King Louis was on board; the ship was filled with French Crusaders. All was in readiness to put to sea.

The captain of the king's ship called to his sailors, "Are you ready?" They answered, "Aye, Sir." "Let the clerks and priests come forward," said the captain. As soon as they had done so he shouted, "Sing, for God's sake!" They immediately chanted the *Veni Creator Spiritus*. Then the captain ordered the seamen, "Spread the sails, for God's sake," and they did so, and in a short time wind filled the sails and bore them out of sight of land.

In 1627 this Latin hymn was translated by an English rector named Cosin, one of the revisers of the *Prayer Book*, who inserted it in the Ordination Service of the Church of England.

In 1738 it was adapted by Charles Wesley for congregational use and published by him in his *Psalms and Hymns*.

In the year 1831, Dr. Blomfield, Bishop of London, was to hold an ordination service at St. Paul's Cathedral. Thomas Attwood was the organist at that time, and he was asked by the bishop if he would compose a tune for use on that special day. Just two days to write it!

The beautiful tune we sing today is the result. Mr. Attwood relates how he put the finishing touches to it on his way to the morning service from his home in the outskirts of London:

> *Come, Holy Ghost, our souls inspire,*
> *And lighten with celestial fire:*
> *Thou, the anointing Spirit art,*
> *Who dost Thy seven-fold gifts impart:*

Thy blessed unction from above
Is comfort, life, and fire of love!
Enable with perpetual light,
The dullness of our blinded sight!

Anoint and cheer our soiled face
With the abundance of Thy grace:
Keep far our foes, give peace at home;
Where Thou art Guide no ill can come.

Teach us to know the Father, Son,
And Thee, of both, to be but one:
That through the ages all along
This may be our endless song.

:-:-:-:

"COME, O THOU TRAVELER UNKNOWN"

UNDER THE title of "Wrestling Jacob" this famous
hymn by Charles Wesley was first published in *Hymns
and Sacred Poems* in 1742. It is held by some authorities to be the greatest of Wesley's hymns. Watts,
who wrote many beautiful hymns, was reputed to have
said of it that it was worth all the verses he had written.
Montgomery, also, thought it very fine. Its deep pathos
was keenly felt by John Wesley, who, very soon after
the death of his brother, was preaching at Bolton, and
gave out this hymn. As he read the lines,

My company before is gone
And I am left alone with Thee,

he sat down in the pulpit and covered his face with
his hands, overcome with emotion and unable to speak.
In the whole congregation there could hardly be found
an eye free from tears. Recovering himself, Wesley

continued the service, which those who took part in it never forgot.

In 1876, Dean Stanley unveiled a memorial to the Wesleys in Westminster Abbey. The dean's wife, Lady Augusta Stanley, had died a little time before, and as the memorial was dedicated the Dean read these memorable words.

A hundred years after its first appearance Charles Wesley's grandson, S. S. Wesley, composed the tune named Peniel for this hymn:

> *Come, O Thou Traveler unknown,*
> *Whom still I hold, but cannot see!*
> *My company before is gone.*
> *And I am left alone with Thee:*
> *With Thee all night I mean to stay,*
> *And wrestle till the break of day.*
>
> *I need not tell Thee who I am,*
> *My misery and sin declare:*
> *Thyself hast called me by my name:*
> *Look on Thy hands, and read it there:*
> *But who, I ask Thee, who art Thou?*
> *Tell me Thy Name and tell me now.*
>
> *In vain Thou strugglest to get free:*
> *I never will unloose my hold!*
> *Art Thou the man that died for me?*
> *The secret of Thy love unfold:*
> *Wrestling, I will not let Thee go,*
> *Till I Thy name, Thy nature know.*

:-:-:-:

"COME, YE DISCONSOLATE"

THOMAS MOORE, the Irish poet, was born in Dublin, 1779, where his father was a well-to-do grocer. His warm and generous spirit began early to express itself as readily in poetry as in prose. While a student at Trinity College he made friends with Robert Emmet, a fiery leader in plots against the government. In 1797 things came to a head and Moore barely escaped being entangled. Emmet was imprisoned, tried, and executed.

These events left a great impression on Moore's mind and tinged his heart with sorrow. He was graduated in 1798, and in the following year left for England to read law. His wit, personality, and charming voice soon won him a place in the drawing-rooms of London Society.

In 1808 *Irish Melodies* was published, which included his tribute to his lost friend Emmet, in the song commencing, "Oh, breathe not his name!" These social activities of Tom Moore were too costly for his pocket and he sank steadily into debt. When his publishers advanced him money, he wrote them songs in payment!

To escape other debts, he accepted an appointment in Bermuda as Registrar of the Prize Court. Soon tiring of this monotonous life, he appointed a deputy to take his place and returned to England by way of the United States and Canada. The Canadian visit inspired him later to write "The Canadian Boat Song" ("Faintly as tolls the evening chime").

In 1807 he was back in Ireland, where he met the lovely actress, Elizabeth Dyke. The famous song, "O believe me if all those endearing young charms" and others almost as popular were inspired by her. They were married in 1811 and went to London to live, moving later to a little house in the country named Mayfield Cottage.

Tom Moore continued to be in request at the great houses of fashion, where he received a warm welcome; this enabled him to replenish his purse. He was often away from home for months at a time, but his home-coming was a happy event. The death of his eldest daughter was a great sorrow for the family; thereafter the sun never seemed to shine quite so brightly for Tom Moore. But worse was in store, for his little daughter Anastasia was sick unto death. He wept in the arms of his wife as they watched together another dear one pass beyond him.

His sensitive and tender spirit was crushed—and saying, "O Bessie, I can't bear it," he sought the open solitude to battle with the terrible sorrow that gripped his heart. Followed—as calmness came—these feeling words, wrung from his inmost being:

Come, ye disconsolate, where'er ye languish;
Come to the mercy-seat, fervently kneel:
Here bring your wounded hearts, here tell your anguish
Earth has no sorrow that heaven cannot heal.

Joy of the desolate, light of the straying,
Hope of the penitent, fadeless and pure,
Here speaks the Comforter, tenderly saying,
Earth has no sorrow that heaven cannot cure.

Here see the bread of life; see waters flowing
Forth from the throne of God, pure from above:
Come to the feast of love, come ever knowing
Earth has no sorrow but heaven can remove.

The last two verses were altered from the original and adapted to suit the hymn-books.

"DEAR LORD AND FATHER OF MANKIND"

IT WAS the year 1819. On the farm at Hampton Falls, New Hampshire, all hands were at work harvesting. The little farm boy was almost run off his feet from early dawn until dark. The lad had no time for anything but work, although only twelve summers had passed since he was born at the little farm shack down the road.

The winters were better for John Whittier, when he and his sister spent the day at the schoolhouse. The evenings were well occupied in "chores." But John was happy enough.

The years slipped by. One day, while working around the farm, he met a peddler, who was singing to his heart's content. John stood to listen: the words gripped him inside, somehow. He asked the man to keep on singing. The peddler persuaded John to buy a book — the works of "Bobbie" Burns. The book opened up another world to him—a world that reached his heart—through words.

John found himself writing verse after his work on the farm, and in the evenings he shyly showed it to his sister, who thought it so good that she sent it to a newspaper edited by William Lloyd Garrison, who was amazed by his genius. Garrison sought out young Whittier and made a friend of him, persuading him eventually to move into his office in the city. John showed great aptitude and talent in his new work and put power into his pen. He soon became a recognized leader.

In 1828 he became editor of the *American Manufacturer;* in 1830, of the *New England Review.*

All his life he used the Quaker speech and dress.

He made his home at Amesbury, Mass., but later lived
at Oak Knoll, Danvers. Whittier wrote many hymns,
although he once said "A hundred years of silence had
taken away their singing."

When he was fifty-three, the "beauty within" enabled
him to write these words:

> *Dear Lord and Father of mankind,*
> *Forgive our foolish ways!*
> *Reclothe us in our rightful mind:*
> *In purer lives Thy service find,*
> *In deeper reverence, praise.*
>
> *In simple trust like theirs who heard*
> *Beside the Syrian sea,*
> *The gracious calling of the Lord—*
> *Let us, like them, without a word*
> *Rise up and follow Thee.*
>
> *O Sabbath rest of Galilee!*
> *O calm of hills above,*
> *Where Jesus knelt to share with thee*
> *The silence of eternity—*
> *Interpreted by love!*
>
> *Drop Thy still dews of quietness,*
> *Till all our striving cease:*
> *Take from our souls the strain and stress,*
> *And let our ordered lives confess*
> *The beauty of Thy peace.*
>
> *Breathe through the heats of our desire*
> *Thy coolness and Thy balm;*
> ***Let sense** be dumb, let flesh retire:*
> *Speak through the earthquake, wind, and fire,*
> *O still small voice of calm!*

Dr. Monk's tune (Campfields) was composed for this
beautiful hymn in first edition of the *Church Hymnary*
(1898).

"FOR ABSENT FRIENDS"

ISABEL STEVENSON was born in Cheltenham in 1843.
The daughter of an army officer, she had an only
brother—to whom she was devoted. The family lived
in Cheltenham and the children were educated there.
Isabel never resided anywhere else.

Both children were delicate in health. As the brother
grew into manhood he was compelled to spend each
winter in a sheltered and sunny part—moving from
one place to another. As the years passed, Isabel became more of a shut-in invalid.

One day the sorrowful news reached her that her
dearly loved brother had been ordered by the doctor
to the dry climate of South Africa. She was much distressed by the leave-taking; and when the day came
for him to sail, a sealed letter was delivered to him
"To be opened at sea." Written on the envelope were
the words, "A Keepsake from Isabel."

Within was a piece of paper on which was written
the following:

> *Holy Father, in Thy mercy*
> *Hear our earnest prayer;*
> *Keep our loved ones, in their absence,*
> *'Neath Thy care.*
>
> *Jesus Savior, let Thy presence*
> *Be their light and guide:*
> *Keep, O keep them, in their weakness,*
> *At Thy side.*
>
> *When in sorrow, when in danger,*
> *When in loneliness,*
> *In Thy love look down and comfort*
> *Their distress.*

May the joy of Thy salvation,
Be their strength and stay:
May they love and may they praise Thee
Day by day.

Holy Spirit, let Thy teaching
Sanctify their life:
Send Thy grace, that they may conquer
In the strife.

Father, Son, and Holy Spirit,
God the One in Three,
Bless them, guide them, save them, keep them,
Near to Thee.

These "touching and lovely lines" were the only ones Miss Stevenson ever wrote. Later these verses were circulated through friends. One came into the possession of an officer of H. M. S. Bacchante, the ship on which his late Majesty King George V and his brother the late Duke of Clarence made their voyage around the world in 1881-2.

It was sung on board at public worship. The royal princes sent a copy home to their mother where it was also sung. The Princess of Wales was especially fond of the words. It was soon included in the hymn books.

"A Prayer for Absent Ones" was a solace for many persons during the Great War.

:-:-:-:

"FOREVER WITH THE LORD"

At Irving, in Ayrshire, a remarkable genius was born in 1771—James Montgomery. His father was a Moravian minister, who, wishing to bring up the boy in the same way, sent him to a Moravian school in Yorkshire. Meanwhile his parents went to the West Indies as missionaries. Both died soon after their arrival and James was alone.

After a little while at the school, James ran away and found employment in a shop at Wakefield. Leaving there, he found work at a little place called Wart-upon-Deane, in a small store, where he was happy. In the evenings and spare time he wrote verse. He said he couldn't help writing. By the time he was eighteen he had quite a collection and was ambitious to have them published.

He gave up his job and went to London, but he failed to get into print. So he went to Sheffield, where he secured work in the office of a newspaper, the Sheffield *Register*. Here he was to stay for over thirty years, rising to become proprietor and changing the name of it to the Sheffield *Iris*. There were times when his ultra-Liberal views clashed with the government for printing forbidden political affairs. He was imprisoned in York Castle and fined.

It was while he was there that some of his best verses were written. From York Castle this inspired genius wrote this immortal hymn:

> *"Forever with the Lord!"*
>   *Amen, so let it be:*
> *Life from the dead is in that word,*
>   *'Tis immortality!*
> *Here in the body pent,*
>   *Absent from Him I roam,*
> *Yet nightly pitch my moving tent*
>   *A day's march nearer home.*

My Father's house on high,
Home of my soul, how near
At times, to faith's unclouded eye,
Thy golden gates appear!
Ah! then my spirit faints
To reach the land I love—
The bright inheritance of saints,
Jerusalem above!

"Forever with the Lord!"
Father, if 'tis Thy will,
The promise of that faithful word
Even here to me fulfil.
Be Thou at my right hand,
Then can I never fail;
Uphold Thou me, and I shall stand,
Fight, and I must prevail.

So when my latest breath
Shall rend the veil in twain,
By death I shall escape from death,
And life eternal gain.
Knowing as I am known,
How shall I love that word,
And oft repeat before the throne,
"Forever with the Lord!"

The government made atonement to **Montgomery** in
after years and conferred a pension upon him.

One day a friend asked him, "Which of your poems
will live?" To which he replied, "None, Sir, except
a few of my hymns." Montgomery's name will never
be forgotten. The beauty of his soul is expressed in:

Prayer is the soul's sincere desire,
Unuttered or expressed—
The motion of a hidden fire
That trembles in the breast.

Montgomery·died in his sleep, 1854. He was **given** a
public funeral, and Sheffield was proud to **erect** a monument to one of her most famous sons.

"FORWARD! BE OUR WATCHWORD"

IN 1871 there was to be a big Diocesan Choral Union at Canterbury. The Rev. J. G. Wood, who was the precentor, was eager to have a good processional hymn for the occasion. Why should it be necessary to look further than the Dean of Canterbury himself for an author and composer?

So Dean Alford was asked if he would take the whole matter in hand. The Dean agreed to do his best and in due course sent along the hymn with his compliments. But now the Precentor was in a quandary, for although the hymn was excellent, it was not quite what was wanted.

So undaunted, Mr. Wood pointed out to the good Dean that he would prefer something stirring and easy to march to. "Would he mind going into his cathedral and march slowly down the aisle and compose to his own steps?"

The kindly Dean did as he was told, and the hymn given was the result. Dean Alford sent the manuscript as bidden but only composed the treble and bass. The harmony Mrs. J. Worthington Bliss added.

The tune, "Smart," was composed in 1872 by Henry Smart and is generally used:

> *"Forward!" be our watchword,*
> *Steps and voices join'd:*
> *Seek the thing before us,*
> *Not a look behind:*
> *Burns the fiery pillar*
> *At our army's head:*
> *Who shall dream of shrinking,*
> *By our Captain led?*

Forward through the desert,
Through the toil and fight:
Jordan flows before us,
Zion beams with light.

Forward, flock of Jesus,
Salt of all the earth,
Till each yearning purpose
Springs to glorious birth:
Sick, they ask for healing,
Blind, they grope for day:
Pour upon the nations
Wisdom's loving ray.
> *Forward, out of error,*
> *Leave behind the night;*
> *Forward through the darkness,*
> *Forward into light!*

To the eternal Father
Loudest anthems raise:
To the Son and Spirit
Echo songs of praise:
To the Lord of glory,
Blessed Three in One,
Be by men and angels
Endless honors done:
> *Weak are earthly praises:*
> *Dull the songs of night:*
> *Forward into triumph,*
> *Forward into light.*

:-:-:-:

"GO BURY THY SORROW"

MARY BACHELOR was staying with her brother, the minister of a west country parish in England. He was a hard-working man. His many poor parishioners found in him a sympathetic and ready listener and poured their troubles into his patient ear. After a busy day round his parish he would have welcomed rest, but Mary always had so much to tell him of her own worries (real and imagined) that even at home there was no repose.

One summer day, after a long talk with her brother about some peculiar trouble she was enduring, she suddenly became aware of a shadow crossing the face of the brother she loved.

As she stood by the open door and looked out upon the garden before her, across the grass lay heavy shadows cast by the tall trees, and as she gazed, there came to her the thought—"That is just what I have done to my brother! Why did I do it? Why did I, not rather hide my own sorrows and allow only cheerfulness to greet him? Why did I not try to cheer him?" Greatly distressed to have carelessly added to the load by the intrusion of her personal difficulties, she wrote:

> Go bury thy sorrow, the world hath its share;
> Go bury it deeply, go, hide it with care!
> Go think of it calmly, when curtained by night
> Go tell it to Jesus, and all will be right.
>
> Go tell it to Jesus, He knoweth thy grief,
> Go tell it to Jesus, He'll send thee relief:
> Go gather the sunshine He sheds on the way:
> He'll lighten thy burden—go weary one—pray.
>
> Hearts growing aweary with heavier woe,
> Now drop 'mid the darkness—go, comfort them—go!
> Go bury thy sorrow, let others be blest:
> Go give them the sunshine, tell Jesus the rest.

Mary showed these lines to her brother, expressing her sorrow for the bother that she had given him. The hymn was printed and sung in his church, whence it was borne farther afield, taking with it a universal note of comfort and cheer to the heavy laden.

:-:-:-:

"GOD BE WITH YOU TILL WE MEET AGAIN!"

JEREMIAH EAMES RANKIN, D.D., LL.D., was born at Thornton, New Hampshire, in 1828, and was educated at Middleburg College, Vermont, and at Andover Theological Seminary. Churches in New York, St. Albans, Charlestown, and Washington, D.C., owe much to his ministry.

Afterwards—when president of Howard University, Washington, he edited the *Gospel Temperance Hymnal,* which had a great following; also *Gospel Bells.* He was a versatile writer and published a book of his own poems entitled *German-English Lyrics, Sacred and Secular,* and contributed many articles to the daily press.

Of all the things he wrote and published, not any are considered now. All are gone but this one hymn, written when he was about fifty-six years of age:

God be with you till we meet again;
By His counsels guide, uphold you,
With His sheep securely fold you;
God be with you till we meet again.

CHORUS
Till we meet, till we meet,
Till we meet at Jesus' feet;
Till we meet, till we meet,
God be with you till we meet again.

God be with you till we meet again;
'Neath His wings securely hide you,
Daily manna still provide you;
God be with you till we meet again.
Chorus

God be with you till we meet again;
When life's perils thick confound you;
Put His arms unfailing round you;
God be with you till we meet again.
Chorus

God be with you till we meet again;
Keep love's banner floating o'er you;
Smite death's threatening wave before you;
God be with you till we meet again.
Chorus

Written when Dr. Rankin was minister of the First Congregational Church, Washington, in 1882, he explained it "as the Christian's good-bye," meaning "God be with you."

The popular and well-known tune was composed by Mr. W. G. Tomer.

:-:-:-:

"GOD MOVES IN A MYSTERIOUS WAY"

"GOD MOVES in a mysterious way" — so wrote William Cowper after much mental suffering. The simple life of Cowper marked by its tender friendships was in reality a tragedy!

He was the only surviving child of the Rev. John Cowper, D.D., Rector of Berkhamstead, Hertford, England. His mother, to whom he was devotedly attached, died when he was only six years of age. His great grief he never forgot, for when he was sixty, he chanced on a picture of his mother. On seeing it, he wrote those exquisite and touching lines, "To My Mother's Picture":

> *O that those lips had language, life has pass'd*
> *With me but roughly since I heard thee last.*

He went to a Dame's School, where he was very unhappy, being of such a sensitive nature that the boys made his life a misery. When he went to Westminster he was happier. He studied law, and during those years fell in love with his cousin. The marriage was forbidden by his father, but the lovers never forgot one another. Fits of melancholy, which had clung to him in his boyhood, began to increase, and on reaching maturity he found himself unable to shake them off.

His father died and he was left in poorer circumstances. Then came the dire calamity that seemed to destroy all hope of advancement. He had been nominated to a post in the House of Lords but the fear of appearing before a committee to show his ability for the office completely upset his mental balance. He had a dark delusion that God had sent him punishment. With kind care this passed away, but the dark cloud followed him at intervals and it was due to this state of mind that we owe this majestic hymn.

One evening in the year 1768 this cloud once more settled upon him. He hired a post chaise to go and drown himself. The night was very dark, with storm, and rain in torrents—the coachman purposely lost his

way, and after a long drive round took him home again.
By this time the mood had lifted. Deeply thankful,
he wrote:

> God moves in a mysterious way
>   His wonders to perform;
> He plants His footsteps in the sea,
>   And rides upon the storm.
>
> Deep in unfathomable mines
>   Of never-failing skill,
> He treasures up His bright designs,
>   And works His sovereign will.
>
> Ye fearful saints, fresh courage take!
>   The clouds ye so much dread
> Are big with mercy, and shall break
>   In blessings on your head.
>
> Judge not the Lord by feeble sense,
>   But trust Him for His grace;
> Behind a frowning providence
>   He hides a smiling face.
>
> His purposes will ripen fast,
>   Unfolding every hour;
> The bud may have a bitter taste,
>   But sweet will be the flower.
>
> Blind unbelief is sure to err,
>   And scan His work in vain;
> God is His own interpreter,
>   And He will make it plain.

:-:-:-:

"HARK! THE GLAD SOUND"

PHILLIP DODDRIDGE was born in 1702, the twentieth
child of well-to-do parents who lived in London. His
grandfather held a living in the Anglican Church, but

under the Act of Uniformity was ejected. His mother's father (a pastor) had to flee from Germany to England, an exile for life. Both his father and mother died when he was a child, and life for him was not happy. He was a lad of great promise. He said in after years that he owed much to his Lutheran mother. Before he was twenty he began to preach.

The bountiful Duchess of Bedford was greatly taken with this gift and offered to send him to Oxford to take Holy Orders. He declined, preferring to be independent.

Doddridge had a great friend in the older man, Watts. They found many things in common, and each had literary attainments. Doddridge had great talent. Watts helped him to publish a noted book of the time, called *Rise and Progress of Religion in the Soul,* a book that was translated into many languages. The great benefactor of slaves, William Wilberforce, said, "It was due to reading this work which brought about in my own life a great spiritual change, enabling me to write my practical view of Christianity" and that, in its turn, was the inspiration of that eminent Scot, Dr. Chalmers.

Though these books are now in oblivion, their influence is maintained in works that remain. The beautiful hymns that Doddridge wrote will not die from neglect. In his lifetime he never saw them in print. He wrote them out by hand on slips of paper, and they were passed round at the service. The clearly written manuscripts are as fresh today as ever, the ink unfaded.

The following hymn was written for his congregation, to herald the coming of Christmas, 1735:

Hark, the glad sound, the Savior comes,
　　The Savior promised long;
Let every heart prepare a throne
　　And every voice a song.

He comes the prisoner to release
　　In Satan's bondage held;
The gates of brass before Him burst,
　　The iron fetters yield.

He comes the broken heart to bind,
　　The bleeding soul to cure,
And with the treasures of His grace,
　　To bless the humble poor.

Our glad hosannas, Prince of peace,
　　Thy welcome shall proclaim;
And Heaven's eternal arches ring,
　　With Thy beloved name.

The tune *Crediton* was composed by Thomas Clark in 1810.

Doddridge remained for more than twenty years at Northampton. He was a kindly and sympathetic man, loved by all with whom he came in contact. His learning was acknowledged by men of note. His health, never good, compelled him to seek a genial climate for the winter months. He sailed for Lisbon and lived just two weeks after his arrival there, dying at the early age of fifty years in 1751.

Doddridge wrote the beautiful hymn sung at Dr. Livingstone's funeral in Westminster Abbey, April, 1874:

O God of Bethel, by whose hand
Thy people still are fed.

:-:-:-:

"HARK! THE HERALD ANGELS SING"

CHARLES WESLEY was educated at Westminster School and Christ Church, Oxford, where he graduated in 1729 and became a college tutor. In 1735, John and Charles Wesley were invited by the famous colonizer, General Oglethorpe, to visit him in Georgia (Charles acted as his secretary). After some time there, they returned to England.

The brothers were inseparable—John the leader, and Charles the hymn-writer, who found it easy to express his thoughts and feelings in hymns and wrote literally thousands of them. As the great festival of Christmas approached in 1739, Charles Wesley wrote this hymn, familiar to all of us:

Hark! the herald angels sing
Glory to the newborn King,
Peace on earth and mercy mild,
God and sinners reconciled.
Joyful all ye nations rise,
Join the triumph of the skies!
With angelic host proclaim
Christ is born in Bethlehem.
Hark! the herald angels sing
Glory to the newborn King.

Christ by highest heaven adored,
Christ the everlasting Lord.
Late in time behold Him come,
Offspring of a virgin's womb.
Veiled in flesh the godhead see!
Hail! the Incarnate Deity!
Pleased as man with man to dwell
Jesus, our Emmanuel,
Hark! the herald angels sing
Glory to the newborn King.

Hail the heaven-born Prince of Peace!
Hail! the Sun of Righteousness,
Light and life to all He brings,
Risen with healing in His wings,
Mild He lays His glory by
Born that man no more may die,
Born to raise the sons of earth,
Born to give them second birth,
Hark! the herald angels sing
Glory to the newborn King.

When the hymn was written it had no chorus, but the music required this, so it was added. There is an interesting story told of how this tune was discovered. "In 1885, Dr. W. H. Cummings, who was the organist at Waltham Abbey, was going over some music of Mendelssohn's, *Festgesang for Male voices and Orchestra,* first performed at Leipzig, June, 1840. He adapted it, copied out the parts, and had the tune sung by the choir at Waltham Abbey. It was received with such favor that it seemed worth while to publish the adaption in 1856, and it soon appeared in many hymn-books." The first to publish it was the Rev. R. R. Chope's Congregational hymn and tune book, entitled *St. Vincent.*

Charles and John Wesley traveled over the country together, chiefly on horseback. In 1756 Charles, never very robust, gave up these jaunts and settled at Bristol, whence he moved to London in 1771. Devoted as he was to his brother, John, he failed to approve of his ordination and often declared that "he had lived and would die in the Communion of the Church of England."

:-:-:-:

"HOLY NIGHT"

THE BELLS of Oberndorf (in Austria) were pealing as the village folk picked their way through the newly fallen snow on Christmas Eve, 1818. The air was crisp, yet not too cold, the frost making a fairyland of the pines. The stars seemed to have a special brightness, twinkling a welcome as the villagers hastened to midnight mass . . . and to pray round the Crib on this joyful night.

There had been rumors of a musical surprise. Father Mohr, the assistant priest—so went the talk—had composed a new carol. He and his talented friend, Franz Gruber, had been working on it all day, but when all was ready for the service the organ would not work. It was falling to pieces. So Gruber sang the melody in a tenor voice, accompanying himself on the guitar, with some assistance from the bass voice of the composer. A few girls from the village formed a choir to sing the chorus.

The little church was filled to the doors with simple folk, who stood in rapt attention to hear sung for the first time:

Holy night! Peaceful night!
All is dark, save the light
Yonder where they sweet vigil keep
O'er the Babe who in silent sleep
Rests in heavenly peace
Rests in heavenly peace.

Holy night! Peaceful night!
Only for Shepherds' sight
Came blest visions of angel throngs
With their loud Alleluia songs
Saying, "Christ is come,"
Saying, "Christ is come."

Holy night! Peaceful night!
Child of heaven, O how bright
Thou didst smile on us when Thou wast born,
Blest indeed was that happy morn,
Full of heavenly joy,
Full of heavenly joy.

There was something in this carol that gripped their hearts and made the tears course down many cheeks— joyful, yet sad—to welcome the Prince of Peace.

Very soon wandering Tyrolese carried this tune over the Alps until it became popular before it was printed and Christmas anywhere was not complete without it.

A chapel built in memory of the composer of this wonderful carol was unveiled by the Austrian Chancellor in August, 1937.

"HOW SWEET THE NAME OF JESUS SOUNDS"

There is a tablet on the wall of St. Mary Woolnoth, Lombard Street, London, that runs:

John Newton
Clerk
Once an infidel and libertine—
A servant of slaves in Africa
was
by the rich mercy of our Lord
and Saviour Jesus Christ
preserved, restored, pardoned
and appointed to preach the faith
he had long laboured to destroy—
Near sixteen years at Olney in
Bucks
And twenty-seven years
in this Church.

This inscription was written by the man whose character it portrayed, at the age of eighty-two, the year of his death.

Born in London, 1725, Newton occupied a unique place among the founders of the Evangelical Church, due to his powerful character and romantic early life.

His mother, a devout Dissenter, had poured into his willing ear stories from the Bible. She died when he was seven. After two years at school—he was about eleven—his father, a sea captain, took the boy on his first voyage. Six years later, on a shore visit, he met and fell in love with a beautiful girl of fourteen named Mary Catlett. They plighted their troth and it was agreed that they were to be married at the conclusion of his next voyage. Fate, however, intervened, for on his way back to his lodgings Newton was seized by the notorious Press Gang and taken aboard a British man-o-war.

After great hardships and suffering, he escaped while the ship lay off the West Indies, but he was brought back and flogged as a deserter. After this he lost his faith in God, and in his own words, "became too vile for the vile company with him."

Once again he escaped, to fall into the hands of a slave dealer in Africa. For fifteen months he lived as a slave and for some years commanded a slave ship. He was now so hard that he was apathetic to any cruelty to the wretched slaves. But his time was near at hand, for in a terrible storm from which he never expected to escape he saw himself as he really was, and begged the Lord for mercy. His ship was nearly lost but eventually they made shore. Newton was now all remorse. He gave up the sea and began to study the classics, coming under the influence of the great evangelists, Whitefield and the Wesleys. In the meantime he had found and married Mary Catlett.

At the age of thirty-nine he was ordained to the Curacy of Olney, Bucks, England. Newton's life was now all zeal for the Master. He met Cowper and formed a life-long friendship with him. Together they wrote the *Olney Hymns*. In this quiet retreat he was given the inspiration to repair his life and was enabled to give to posterity this sublime hymn:

How sweet the Name of Jesus sounds
In a believer's ear!
It soothes his sorrows, heals his wounds,
And drives away his fear.

It makes the wounded spirit whole
And calms the troubled breast:
'Tis manna to the hungry soul,
And to the weary rest.

Dear Name, the rock on which I build,
My shield and hiding-place.
My never-failing treasury filled
With boundless stores of grace.

Jesus! my shepherd, guardian, friend,
My prophet, priest, and King:
My Lord, my life, my way, my end,
Accept the praise I bring.

Weak is the effort of my heart
And cold my warmest thought:
But when I see Thee as Thou art
I'll praise Thee as I ought.

Till then I would Thy love proclaim
With every fleeting breath:
And may the music of Thy Name
Refresh my soul in death.

"I HEARD THE VOICE OF JESUS SAY"

THE GREAT Scottish Presbyterian, Dr. Bonar, was the son of a lawyer. He was born in Edinburgh and educated there. In later life he declared that he owed much to the influence of three famous men — Dr. Chalmers, Edward Irving, and Murray McCheyne.

As a young man he began his ministry at St. John's Church, Leith. It was for the Sunday school there that he wrote his first hymn, "I Lay My Sins on Jesus." This was set to a jaunty air and printed in leaflet form. The children liked to sing a hymn to a tune they knew, and Sunday school became more popular in consequence.

In 1837 he moved to Kelso, where he worked for twenty-nine years, loved and revered by all classes. It was at Kelso that he wrote many of his well known hymns. At that time a paraphrase of the Psalms was the "Song of Praise" in the *Kirk*. The service was more one of prayer than of song.

During the first visit of Moody and Sankey in the Assembly Hall, Edinburgh, in 1873, the singing of a hymn had just been completed, when a shrill voice was heard at the door calling, "Let me oot! Let me oot! What would John Knox say to the likes o' yon?" Sankey himself said about his first visit to Scotland that he was not quite sure how they would take to solo singing! It had never been countenanced in the *kirk!* But on this particular and important occasion, Dr. Bonar was to be present—"And of all men's opinions," relates Mr. Sankey, "I wanted his." (Bonar's own beautiful hymns had never been sung in his own *kirk*.) "So on taking my seat at the organ I was overjoyed to see him in the front seat. I felt the solemnity of

this moment, but believing in the truth contained in
the hymn, I sang it to the end.   Never did I experience
such silence!"   At the close of the service, Dr. Bonar
reached out his hand and said, "Mr. Sankey, you sang
the gospel tonight."   A tale told in song had come
to stay.

Dr. Bonar was about thirty-eight when he wrote the
following hymn.   It was printed in 1846.   Twenty-two
years afterwards, the talented Dr. Dykes composed
the unforgettable tune, which is a general favorite:

> I heard the voice of Jesus say,
> "Come unto Me and rest:
> Lay down, thou weary one, lay down
> Thy head upon My breast!"
> I came to Jesus as I was:
> Weary, and worn, and sad:
> I found in Him a resting-place,
> And He has made me glad.
>
> I heard the voice of Jesus say,
> "Behold, I freely give
> The living water, thirsty one,
> Stoop down, and drink, and live."
> I came to Jesus, and I drank
> Of that life-giving stream:
> My thirst was quenched, my soul revived,
> And now I live in Him.
>
> I heard the voice of Jesus say,
> "I am this dark world's Light:
> Look unto Me, thy morn shall rise,
> And all thy day be bright."
> I look'd to Jesus, and I found
> In Him my star, my sun:
> And in that Light of life I'll walk
> Till traveling days are done.

"IN THE SWEET BY AND BY"

Early in 1860 S. Fillmore Bennett was living in
the village of Elkhorn, Wisconsin. He had a great
friend by the name of Joseph P. Webster, who was
musical to the tips of his fingers but was tormented
with a highly nervous, sensitive nature. Bennett recognized all the "sign-posts" of his friend's nature and
knew immediately when he saw him exactly how he was
feeling. He would try all inducements to get him out
of a melancholy mood. One method was to request
a tune for a song he had written. One day Webster
came into his friend's house and stood by the fire,
leaning on the mantle-piece, most despondent. Mr.
Bennett related:

" 'Webster,' I said, 'What is the matter now?' 'It
is no matter,' he replied; 'It will be all right by and
by.' The idea came to me like a flash of sunlight, and
I replied, 'The sweet by and by! Would not that make
a good hymn?' 'Maybe it would,' said he indifferently.
Turning to the desk, I penned the three verses and
chorus as fast as I could write. In the meantime two
friends had come in. I handed the hymn to Mr.
Webster. As he read it his eye kindled and his whole
demeanor changed. Stepping to the desk, he started
to write the notes in a moment, and taking up his violin
played over the melody. In a few moments more he
had the notes for the four parts of the chorus jotted
down. I think it was not more than thirty minutes
from the time I took up my pen to write the words
before the two friends, Webster and myself, were singing the hymn in the same form in which it was afterwards published and became popular. While singing,
another friend entered, and, after listening awhile,

with tears in his eyes, uttered the prediction, 'That hymn is immortal.'"

It was first published in a book of songs called *The Signet Ring* issued soon after the American Civil War. It is now in many collections and has been translated into various foreign languages and is sung in almost every land under the sun.

> *There's a land that is fairer than day,*
> *And by faith we can see it afar,*
> *For the Father waits over the way,*
> *To prepare us a dwelling-place there.*
>
> > *In the sweet by and by*
> > *We shall meet on that beautiful shore,*
> > *In the sweet by and by*
> > *We shall meet on that beautiful shore.*
>
> *We shall sing on that beautiful shore:*
> *The melodious songs of the blest,*
> *And our spirits shall sorrow no more,*
> *Not a sigh for the blessing of rest.*
> > Chorus
>
> *To our bountiful Father above*
> *We will offer our tribute of praise,*
> *For the glorious gift of His love,*
> *And the blessings that hallow our days.*
> > Chorus

:-:-:-:

"I NEED THEE EVERY HOUR"

THE WRITER of this hymn was Mrs. Hawks. She was born in New York and lived for some years in Brooklyn, where she attended the Baptist Church of which the musical Dr. Robert Lowry was the pastor.

She was fond of writing poems and many of her works were printed in Sunday school hymn-books.

Dr. Lowry encouraged her to write and set some of the compositions to music, but this is her only note-worthy hymn. It came out first in a small edition of *Gospel Songs*, gathered together by the National Baptist Sunday school Association, which met in Cincinnati, November, 1872, and was sung there. When Mrs. Hawks wrote this work, she had not felt any great sorrow. She had a happy home and was surrounded by those she loved.

Writing in 1895 to a friend, she said: "I remember well the morning more than twenty years ago, when in a distant city, I was so filled with a sense of near-ness to the Master that, wondering how one could live without Him, either in joy or pain, these words, 'I need Thee every hour,' were flashed into my mind, the thought taking full possession of me. Seating myself by the open windows in the balmy air of the bright June day, I caught my pencil, and the words were soon committed to paper, almost as they are being sung now. It was only by accident, as it would seem, that they were set to music a few months later and sung for the first time at a Sunday school Convention held in one of the large Western cities of America. From there they were taken farther west and sung by thousands of voices, before the echo came back to me, thrilling my heart with surprise and gladness. For myself the hymn was prophetic rather than expressive of my own experiences at the time it was written, and I did not understand why it so touched the great throbbing heart of hu-manity.

"It was not until long years after when the shadow

fell over my way—the shadow of a great loss—that I understood something of the comforting words which I had been permitted to give out to others in my hours of sweet security and peace.

"Now when I hear them sung, as I have sometimes by hundreds of voices in chorus, I find it difficult to realize that they were ever consciously my own thoughts or penned by my own hand."

Mrs. Hawks died at Bennington, Vermont, in 1918.

> *I need Thee every hour,*
> *Most gracious Lord:*
> *No tender voice like Thine*
> *Can peace afford.*
> *I need Thee, O I need Thee,*
> *Every hour I need Thee,*
> *O bless me now, my Savior,*
> *I come to Thee.*
>
> *I need Thee every hour,*
> *Stay Thou near by:*
> *Temptations lose their power*
> *When Thou art nigh.*
> *I need Thee, O I need Thee,*
>   *Chorus*
>
> *I need Thee every hour,*
> *In joy or pain:*
> *Come quickly and abide*
> *Or life is vain.*
> *I need Thee, O I need Thee,*
>   *Chorus*
>
> *I need Thee every hour,*
> *Teach me Thy will:*
> *And Thy rich promises*
> *In me fulfil.*
> *I need Thee, O I need Thee,*
>   *Chorus*

"I THINK WHEN I READ THAT SWEET STORY OF OLD"

IN THE CASE of most of our hymns, it has been the story first and afterwards the music, but this particular hymn was the exception. Mrs. Luke tells the story in her pleasing book of her life:

"Miss Thompson had made up her mind to be a missionary, but when a severe illness prevented, she turned her talents to teaching and editing a child's missionary magazine. In 1841, Miss Thompson was taking a course in teaching at an infants' school in the Gray's Inn Road, London. Her friend, Mary Moffat, was there also (afterwards Mrs. Livingstone). In the course of their duties, the teachers used to march up and down the schoolroom singing their marching pieces for future use. Amongst these was a Greek air which greatly took Jemima's fancy. She searched in vain for the tune—then she was suddenly called home to go on a visit to Taunton (Somerset).

"While there, she had to go one day to a little town—one hour's ride on the stage-coach. It was a beautiful spring morning. As she waited for the coach to pick her up, she found that she was the only passenger. So, taking an old envelope she penciled off a couple of verses to match the Greek tune that so intrigued her. They were:

> *I think when I read that sweet story of old*
> *When Jesus was here among men,*
> *How He called little children as lambs to His fold,*
> *I should like to have been with Him then.*
> *I wish that His hands had been placed on my head*
> *That His arms had been thrown around me*
> *That I might have seen His kind look when He said,*
> *"Let the little ones come unto Me."*

Yet still to His footstool in prayer I may go
  And ask for a share in His love:
And if I now earnestly seek Him below,
  I shall see Him and hear Him above.
In that beautiful place He has gone to prepare
  For all who are washed and forgiven,
And many dear children are gathering there,
  For of such is the kingdom of heaven.

This was as far as she got when the coach stopped
with a jolt. She had arrived already! She put the
verses away, meaning to repeat them to the village
Sunday school. She gave them the name of "The
Child's Desire." Mrs. Luke (as the authoress became)
wrote also in her memoirs: "My father superintended
the Sunday school at the little chapel belonging to the
estate; he used to let the children choose the first hymn
themselves. One Sunday they struck up this new tune.
My father turned to my younger sister who stood near
him and said, 'Where did that come from? I never
heard it before.' 'Oh, Jemina made it,' was the reply.
On the day following he asked me for a copy of the
words and tune. This he sent with the name and address in full to the Sunday School Teacher's magazine
where it appeared the following month.

"But for my father's intervention the hymn would
in all probability never have been preserved. I added
the third verse to make it a missionary hymn":

But thousands and thousands who wander and fall,
  Never heard of that heavenly home:
I should like them to know there is room for them all
  And that Jesus has bid them to come.
I long for the joy of that glorious time
  The sweetest, and brightest, and best,
When the dear little children of every clime,
  Shall crowd to His arms to be blest.

This hymn of childhood's days bringing many loved scenes to the older generation and ever new to the young, was composed by Miss Jemina Thompson, who was born in 1813, daughter of Thomas Thompson, of Poundsford Park, one of the founders of the British and Foreign Sailors' Society.

In 1843, she married the Rev. Samuel Luke, a Congregational minister of Clifton, but although Mrs. Luke lived to be ninety-three, she did not write another hymn that is remembered.

:-:-:-:

"JESUS BIDS US SHINE"

WHO AMONG the older generation does not remember that once popular book, *The Wide, Wide World*, by Susan Warner, under the pen name of "Elizabeth Wetherell"? Susan was born in New York in 1819. Her father, a well-to-do lawyer, gave his two children (Susan and Ann) a good education to fit them for the social activities of the times. But the sisters, being of a literary turn of mind, exercised their talent in a practical way by teaching in Sunday school, training the young mind to seek good.

Then one day calamity shook their home to its foundations. Their father died. They were penniless. The girls at once started writing to keep the home going, choosing Bible stories as subjects, with characters out of the Old Testament. These had a wide sale, and others were in demand.

Financial problems were not immediately solved, for

money was needed daily and was not always forth-
coming, but neither Susan nor Ann allowed misfor-
tune to dampen their deep trust in God. Then Susan's
book was published, an instant success. It became the
next best seller to *Uncle Tom's Cabin*.

Susan published at least five other books, besides
religious small books for young people. And not the
least of her works for children was the lovely hymn
that appeared in "The Little Corporal" (Chicago):

> *Jesus bids us shine*
> *With a clear, pure light,*
> *Like a little candle*
> *Burning in the night.*
> *In this world of darkness;*
> *So we must shine,*
> *You in your small corner,*
> *And I in mine.*
>
> *Jesus bids us shine,*
> *First of all for Him;*
> *Well He sees and knows it,*
> *If our light grows dim;*
> *He looks down from heaven*
> *He sees us shine,*
> *You in your small corner,*
> *And I in mine.*
>
> *Jesus bids us shine,*
> *Then, for all around;*
> *Many kinds of darkness*
> *In the world are found.*
> *Sin and want, and sorrow:*
> *So we must shine*
> *You in your small corner,*
> *And I in mine.*

Susan Warner died when she was sixty-six and was buried at West Point, not far from her loved home where most of her books were written and where she had a Bible class for the cadets of the United States Military Academy.

:-:-:-:

"JESUS, LOVER OF MY SOUL"

IT WAS an old-fashioned house in which Charles Wesley was living in 1739. One day he was sitting writing at his desk, with the large casement windows of the study flung wide open. There was nothing to disturb his thoughts on such a beautiful day, except the drowsy hum of the bees among the flowers near by. He glanced up from his paper thoughtfully, when there was a sudden flutter by the window, as a frightened bird flew in and, circling the room, settled on his shoulder. He could feel it trembling and took it between his hands gently, stroking its feathers.

Going to the open window, he immediately saw the reason of the little bird's fright, in a hawk hovering attentively overhead. Its intended prey had flown in for refuge.

Putting the bird in a safe place, Wesley returned to his desk and there and then penned this beautiful hymn:

> *Jesus, Lover of my soul,*
> *Let me to Thy bosom fly,*
> *While the nearer waters roll,*
> *While the tempest still is high;*

Hide me, O my Savior, hide,
  Till the storm of life is past:
Safe into the haven guide,
  O receive my soul at last.

Other refuge have I none,
  Hangs my helpless soul on Thee:
Leave, ah, leave me not alone,
  Still support and comfort me:
All my trust on Thee is stayed,
  All my help from Thee I bring:
Cover my defenseless head
  With the shadow of Thy wing.

Thou, O Christ, art all I want!
  More than all in Thee I find:
Raise the fallen, cheer the faint,
  Heal the sick, and lead the blind.
Just and holy is Thy name,
  I am all unrighteousness,
Vile and full of sin I am,
  Thou art full of truth and grace.

Plenteous grace with Thee is found,
  Grace to cover all my sin;
Let the healing streams abound,
  Make and keep me pure within:
Thou of life the fountain art,
  Freely let me take of Thee;
Spring Thou up within my heart,
  Rise to all eternity.

Charles Wesley, of immortal memory, perhaps the most inspired writer of any age, was the youngest son of Samuel and Susannah Wesley, the brother of the saintly John, who, when they were at Oxford were called "The Methodists."

The hymn was first printed in *Hymns and Sacred Poems* in 1740. It was some ten years after his death

that the *Methodist Hymn Book* included it in their
original publication—1797.

Hollingside was the tune that Dr. Dykes composed
in 1861, which was the name of his home, Hollingside
Cottage, about a mile or so from Durham Cathedral,
where he was at the organ.

:-:-:-:

"JESUS, TENDER SHEPHERD, HEAR ME"

As a child, Mary Lundy was called "The bonnie
wee bairnie at the Manse." She was born at Kelso,
Scotland, in 1814, where her father, the Rev. Robert
Lundy, was the minister. During her school days,
Mary showed marked talent for writing verse, putting
daily happenings and letters home into rhyme. When
she was twenty she had several poems of merit to her
name and always hoped to publish a book.

At twenty-two Mary met and married the Rev. William Wallace Duncan, a young minister who had the
Parish of Cleish, Kinrosshire. The lovely Mary, for
her sweet and gentle disposition, was a general favorite,
so the whole parish came to the wedding and showered
upon the young people their affectionate good wishes
and fond farewells.

Mary had spent three happy years in her new home
with a little family growing up round her. Her chief
ambition was for their welfare in all things. At odd
times she wrote poems, putting them away in her desk.
In the late summer of 1839 she wrote a special hymn
for her own children. She put that away also for
future use.

Three months afterwards she was dead of pneumonia!
Going over her papers, her mother found this last beautiful hymn:

> *Jesus, tender Shepherd, hear me,*
>   *Bless Thy little lamb tonight;*
> *Through the darkness be Thou near me,*
>   *Keep me safe till morning light.*
>
> *Through this day Thy hand has led me*
>   *And I thank Thee for Thy care;*
> *Thou hast warmed me, clothed me, fed me,*
>   *Listen to my evening prayer.*
>
> *Let my sins be all forgiven,*
>   *Bless the friends I love so well;*
> *Take me, when I die, to heaven,*
>   *Happy there with Thee to dwell.*

Her mother published this and other poems *In
Memoriam.*

:-:-:-:

"JESUS, THE VERY THOUGHT OF THEE"

ST. BERNARD OF CLAIRVAUX was born in 1091, the
son of a knight who took part in the First Crusade and
did not return. Turning to the monastic life, the young
man entered the Monastery of Citeaux. His talents
were soon recognized. His capable and austere character distinguished by sincerity of purpose made him
a leader of affairs. In due course he was chosen head
of the famous Abbey of Clairvaux, a pivotal position
which brought with it power and influence.

Bernard attracted multitudes to church to listen to
his golden voice, his persuasive and eloquent preaching.
His people loved him. Many of his sermons (in Latin)
have been preserved. The manuscripts may still be
seen. In the eleventh century, long poems were fash-
ionable. Bernard wrote one, parts of which have been
put into hymn form. The one given was a great fa
vorite of Dr. Livingstone, who said "that it used to
ring in his ears as he wandered across the wilds of
the wilderness."

After eight hundred years—in 1854—the Rev. E.
Caswall translated these fine verses, and Dr. Dykes
added the beautiful and haunting refrain, St. Agnes,
Durham:

> *Jesus, the very thought of Thee,*
> *With sweetness fills the breast:*
> *But sweeter far Thy face to see,*
> *And in Thy presence rest.*
>
> *No voice can sing, no heart can frame*
> *Nor can the memory find*
> *A sweeter sound than Jesus' name,*
> *The Savior of mankind.*
>
> *O hope of every contrite heart,*
> *O joy of all the meek,*
> *To those who ask, how kind Thou art!*
> *How good, to those who seek!*
>
> *But what to those who find? Ah this*
> *Nor tongue nor pen can show;*
> *The love of Jesus what it is*
> *None but His loved ones know.*
>
> *Jesus, our only joy be Thou,*
> *As Thou our prize will be:*
> *In Thee be all our glory now*
> *And through eternity.*

In this same long poem are the following hymns, of which we give first lines:
"Jesus, Thou joy of loving hearts"
"O Jesus, King most wonderful"
"Light of the anxious heart"

:-:-:-:

"JERUSALEM THE GOLDEN"

BERNARD OF CLUNY lived in the twelfth century, of Anglo-Saxon stock. He crossed the channel and en-tered the monastery at Cluny, of the great Benedictine house of France, at about the time that King Stephen was precariously holding his English throne. Barons and their retainers were at war there with each other and would swoop down upon some flourishing home-stead and lay waste the land. The powerful barons, like modern gangsters, exacted from the humble tiller of the soil most of his harvest, adding a new hazard to cultivation. Many tales of horror were recounted to the good monks of Cluny, and some of these Bernard recorded.

Nothing much is known of him, except that he wrote a very long Latin poem called "De Contemptu Mundi," much of which consists of scathing rhyme on the wicked-ness of the age and the infamy of men in Stephen's day. In 1851 Dr. J. M. Neale translated this poem, written by the good monk Bernard over seven hundred years before. He took from this long verse three groups, the first contrasting the brevity of this life with the promise of eternity:

> *Brief life is here our portion,*
> *Brief sorrow, short-lived care,*
> *The life that knows no ending*
> *The tear-less life is there.*

The second, Bernard's heart bleeding for the wrongs
of his country:

> *For thee, O dear, dear country,*
> *Mine eyes their vigils keep:*
> *For very love beholding*
> *Thy happy name, they weep.*

And ending the long poem with the sublime dream
of the heavenly land:

> *Jerusalem the golden*
> *With milk and honey blest:*
> *Beneath thy contemplation*
> *Sink heart and voice oppressed:*
> *I know not, O I know not*
> *What joys await me there,*
> *What radiancy of glory,*
> *What bliss beyond compare.*
>
> *They stand, those halls of Zion,*
> *All jubilant with song,*
> *And bright with many an angel*
> *And all the martyr throng:*
> *The Prince is ever with them,*
> *The daylight is serene,*
> *The pastures of the blessed*
> *Are decked in glorious sheen.*
>
> *There is the throne of David,*
> *And there, from care released,*
> *The shout of them that triumph,*
> *The song of them that feast!*
> *And they, who with their leader*
> *Have conquered in the fight,*
> *Forever and forever*
> *Are clad in robes of white.*

O sweet and blessed country,
The home of God's elect:
O sweet and blessed country,
That eager hearts expect:
Jesus in mercy bring us
To that dear land of rest:
Who art with God the Father
And spirit ever blest.

Turning from the devastation around him, Bernard remarked: "Unless the spirit of wisdom and understanding had flowed in upon me, I could not have put together so long a work" (circa 1145). The lovely tune we sing (Ewing) was composed by a paymaster in the Royal Navy.

:-:-:-:

"JUST AS I AM"

A HYMN IS a sacred lyric. It is poetry springing from deep feeling, and it is not unnatural that some of the sweetest hymns have been written by women.

Everybody knows the hymns running: "My God, my Father, while I stray!" and "Christian, seek not yet repose." How many know that the author of both was Charlotte Elliot and that she wrote: "Just as I am, without one plea"—the hymn that is said to have been used to bring more souls into the kingdom of God than any other! Miss Elliott was forty-five when she wrote it. The story of its composition is told by the late Dr. Moule, Bishop of Durham, a relative by marriage.

At the time Miss Elliot was staying with her brother

at Brighton. The household had all gone out to prepare for a bazaar, all, that is, except Charlotte Elliot,
who was an invalid and could take no part.

She was lying on the sofa, feeling her lack of use-
fulness. Her mind turned to ponder over the time
when some twelve years before, a noted evangelist
named Dr. Malan had been a visitor to her father's
house. She remembered the deep impression he had
made upon her and how she had since kept the memory
of that day as her soul's awakening. She began to
feel most grateful for all her blessings — a sudden
feeling of peace and resignation—and wrote the hymn
in full, without effort:

> *Just as I am—without one plea,*
> *But that Thy blood was shed for me,*
> *And that Thou bidd'st me come to Thee—*
> *O Lamb of God, I come.*
>
> *Just as I am—and waiting not*
> *To rid my soul of one dark blot—*
> *To Thee, whose blood can cleanse each spot,*
> *O Lamb of God, I come.*
>
> *Just as I am—poor, wretched, blind;*
> *Sight, riches, healing of the mind—*
> *Yea, all I need, in Thee to find,*
> *O Lamb of God, I come.*
>
> *Just as I am—Thou wilt receive,*
> *Wilt welcome, pardon, cleanse, relieve,*
> *Because Thy promise I believe*
> *O Lamb of God, I come.*
>
> *Just as I am—Thy love unknown*
> *Has broken every barrier down,*
> *Now, to be Thine, yea, Thine alone—*
> *O Lamb of God, I come.*

Just as I am—of that free love
The breadth, length, depth, and height to prove,
Here for a season, Thou above,
O Lamb of God, I come.

The hymn was shown to the family when they returned, and from that shut-in room came to be set down in print and sung in almost every European language.

:-:-:-:

"LEAD KINDLY LIGHT"

THE AUTHOR, John Henry Newman, born February, 1811, was the son of a banker. At seventy-six he was a cardinal of the Roman Church. He graduated at nineteen from Trinity College, Oxford, and was appointed a fellow and tutor of Oriel. In the years following he was troubled by the unrest kindled by the Oxford Movement and underwent a spiritual change which culminated in his joining the Roman Church at the age of forty-four. The hymn has been thought to have been a cry for personal guidance at a time when he had almost decided to renounce his Anglican faith.

Who has not felt the charm of this lovely hymn written on an orange boat westbound for Marseilles? The brilliant and sensitive young minister, stranded in Italy, and now becalmed on a breathless sea. The rough boat, the limp sails, an idle crew waiting for the breeze!

The hymn was written on a Sunday. What greater contrast could there be with the composition of the familiar tune to it, which came to Dr. John B. Dykes as he walked through the busy Strand in London! He had the verse in mind and the tune reached him through the noise and bustle of a crowded street.

A friend visiting Cardinal Newman related:

"I mentioned his well known hymn which he said he wrote when a very young man and was more than thankful for it. 'But, you see,' said he, 'it is not the hymn, but the tune that has won popularity.' "

Lead, Kindly Light, amid the encircling gloom,
Lead Thou me on;
The night is dark, and I am far from home.
Lead Thou me on.
Keep Thou my feet; I do not ask to see
The distant scene: one step enough for me.

I was not ever thus, nor prayed that Thou
Should'st lead me on;
I loved to choose and see my path; but now
Lead Thou me on.
I loved the garish day, and spite of fears,
Pride ruled my will: remember not past years.

So long Thy power hath blessed me, sure it still
Will lead me on
O'er moor and fen, o'er crag and torrent till
The night is gone:
And with the morn those angel faces smile
Which I have loved long since and lost awhile.

"LORD JESUS, THINK ON ME"

IN THE YEAR 375 A.D. there was born to a noble family of Cyrene a son who was named Synesius. In due course he was sent to finish his education at Alexandria, where he attended the popular lectures of the famous Hypatia, whose beauty, goodness, and learning, attracted crowds from all parts of the Eastern world.

Although Synesius was greatly fascinated by Hypatia's pagan philosophy, on his return home he became a Christian and was baptized at the age of twenty-six. He lived the life of a country gentleman, loving sport and the open air. He was very popular, and when his community was attacked, he successfully took the field with a corps of defenders.

He was consecrated Bishop of Ptolemais by acclamation of the people, who loved their volatile, restless, and kindly over-lord. He was not in any sense of the word an ascetic, but was motivated by a benevolent spirit. On his appointment as bishop he refused to give up his wife (as the custom was). A man of unflinching courage in a ruthless world!

Although he wrote a number of odes, this is the only one to descend to posterity. It was born of sorrow and suffering. At the time it was written the bishop was living on his depleted ancestral estate. His lands had been pillaged by warring factions, his people taken into captivity, and their homes set on fire after every male had been killed. His loved wife was dead, and he had just buried his surviving child. His friend, Augustine, was far away. His people had fled. Except for a handful of retainers he was alone.

He wrote an ode to bring comfort to his heart. It was his last writing. Following is an extract.

> Lord Jesus, think on me,
>   And purge away my sin;
> From earth born passions set me free
>   And make me pure within.

Lord Jesus, think on me
With many a care opprest;
Let me Thy loving servant be,
And taste Thy promised rest.

Lord Jesus, think on me,
Nor let me go astray;
Through darkness and perplexity
Point Thou the heavenly way.

Lord Jesus, think on me,
That when the flood is past,
I may the Eternal Brightness see
And share Thy joy at last.

Lord Jesus, think on me,
That I may sing above
Praise to the Father and to Thee
And to the Heavenly Dove.

In 1876 Mr. Chatfield brought out a book of *Songs and Hymns of the Earliest Greek Christian Poets, Bishops, and Others,* translations from the original, in which we find this hymn.

:-:-:-:

"LORD, I HEAR OF SHOWERS OF BLESSING"

ELIZABETH CODNER was the wife of an English Church clergyman. When her husband died she went to live near her friends in the north of London and helped in that busy parish. After some years of work there, she went to Weston-Super-Mare, a little seaside town near Bristol.

Among her many activities in her new home, she edited a monthly magazine—*Woman's Work.* Also she

wrote some small books, chiefly to do with women and
their work.   Besides, she took classes for girls, always
showing concern in the daily life of her pupils and
helping them in many ways.

About this time, 1861, there was great interest in
revival meetings in Ireland.   Branch meetings were
held in London.   Some of her girls had been to one
of these gatherings when in town and came to visit her,
telling her all about the wonderful happenings.   She
thought over this a great deal and was eager that all
the girls should receive a share of the blessing.

The next Sunday, not feeling equal to taking her
usual class, she stayed thoughtfully indoors, with her
writing materials near by.   Without the slightest effort
on her part, these words seemed to be put into her heart
and to flow from her pen:

> Lord, I hear of showers of blessing,
>   Thou art scattering full and free,
> Showers the thirsty land refreshing:
>   Let some drops descend on me—
>   Even me.
>
> Pass me not, O gracious Father,
>   Sinful though my heart may be:
> Thou might'st leave me, but the rather
>   Let Thy mercy light on me—
>   Even me.
>
> Pass me not, O tender Savior:
>   Let me love and cling to Thee;
> I am longing for Thy favor:
>   Whilst Thou'rt calling, O call me—
>   Even me.

Pass me not, O mighty Spirit,
Thou canst make the blind to see:
Witnesser of Jesus' merit,
Speak the word of power to me—
            Even me.

Pass me not; but, pardon bringing,
Bind my heart, O Lord, to Thee:
Whilst the streams of life are springing
Blessing others, O bless me—
            Even me.

She wrote the hymn for the girls of her own circle, never expecting it to go beyond—but being frequently asked for more copies she had them printed and distributed.

Moody and Sankey made the hymn popular during their mission. Sankey gave the words a most plaintive and tender appeal. He related that one woman wrote, "Sir, thank you for singing that hymn . . . Friendless I was in the crowd. . . . I came the next day, and when you got to 'Blessing others, O bless me,' it seemed to reach my very soul and has changed my life. . . . 'Even me.' "

:-:-:-:

"MY FAITH LOOKS UP TO THEE"

My faith looks up to Thee,
Thou Lamb of Calvary,
    Savior divine:
Now hear me when I pray,
Take all my sins away,
O let me from this day
    Be wholly Thine.

SO RUNS the first verse of this beautiful hymn, which is loved by millions of people, sung in many lands and languages. It was written by a young American Congregational minister, Rev. Ray Palmer, when he was twenty-two years old.

One day in 1830 Mr. Palmer was sitting in the quiet of his little room away from the noise and bustle of crowded surroundings. He was thinking deeply of many personal problems which seemed to overwhelm him, and he was discouraged. On a sudden inspiration he took out his notebook and there and then wrote this hymn and put it away without having shown it to anyone. He forgot about it.

Some years after, in Boston, he met Dr. Lowell Mason in the street. Dr. Mason asked him if he would compose a hymn for a new *Hymn and Tune* book about to be published. Palmer suddenly thought of the hymn he had written years before! They went to a quiet nook together where he made a copy from his notebook and gave it to Dr. Mason, who took it home with him. When he read it later he was so pleased that he wrote the well-known tune, Olivet, for it.

Some little time passed and the two men again met on the street. Scarcely waiting to greet his friend, Dr. Mason enthusiastically said, "Mr. Palmer, you may do many things; you may live many years, but you will be known to posterity as the man who wrote, 'My Faith Looks Up to Thee!' "

> *When ends life's transient dream,*
> *When death's cold sullen stream*
> * Shall o'er me roll.*
> *Blest Savior then in love,*
> *Fear and distrust remove:*
> *O bear me safe above,*
> * A ransomed soul.*

"MY GOD, I THANK THEE, WHO HAST MADE"

WHEN CHARLES DICKENS was editor of *Household Words* he had three particular friends—Charles Lamb, Leigh Hunt, and Byron Walter Proctor, better known to the public under the nom de plume, "Barry Cornwall." The three used often to meet and spend a convivial evening. Dickens was particularly happy at the home of the Proctors . . . they had an only daughter who was an accomplished musician and linguist.

In 1858 *Household Words* received a contribution signed "Mary Berwick." Dickens thought the poem was sent by his old governess under an assumed name. The lines were beautiful, and he published them without hesitation. They were:

> *My God, I thank Thee who hast made*
> *The earth so bright,*
> *So full of splendor and of joy,*
> *Beauty and light:*
> *So many glorious things are here,*
> *Noble and right.*
>
> *I thank Thee too that Thou hast made*
> *Joy to abound:*
> *So many gentle thoughts and deeds*
> *Circling us round,*
> *That in the darkest spot of earth*
> *Some love is found.*
>
> *I thank Thee more that all our joy*
> *Is touched with pain:*
> *That shadows fall on brightest hours*
> *That thorns remain.*
> *So that earth's bliss may be our guide*
> *And not our chain.*

For Thou who knowest, Lord, how soon
Our weak heart clings,
Hast given us joys, tender and true,
Yet all with wings:
So that we see, gleaming on high,
Diviner things.

I thank Thee, Lord, that Thou hast kept
The best in store,
We have enough, yet not too much
To long for more:
A yearning for a deeper peace
Not known before.

I thank Thee, Lord, that here our souls
Though amply blest
Can never find, although they seek
A perfect rest:
Nor ever shall, until they lean
On Jesus' breast.

The same "Mary Berwick" contributed other poems
for nearly two years. One particular occasion Dickens
was spending the evening with the Proctors, and during
conversation remarked how much a certain poem by
Mary Berwick had touched his heart. "Oh," said Mr.
Proctor, "I must tell you the secret! Adelaide is Mary
Berwick!"

Dickens was astonished and delighted. The blushing
Adelaide was brought into the drawing-room to receive
the praise of the man whom she had feared would
reject her work. Of Adelaide Proctor, the lovely and
accomplished daughter of his friend, Dickens wrote:
"Now it was the visitation of the sick that had possession of her; now it was the sheltering of the homeless;
now it was the elementary teaching of the densely ig-

norant; now it was the raising up of those who had
wandered and had got trodden underfoot; now it was
the wider employment of her own sex in the general
business of life; now it was all these things at once.
Perfectly unselfish, swift to sympathize, and eager to
relieve, she wrought at such designs with a flushed
earnestness that disregarded season, weather, time of
day or night, food, rest.   Under the strain of such
labors her health broke down, and after fifteen months
of suffering she died in her mother's arms, saying 'It
has come at last.' "

:-:-:-:

"NEARER, MY GOD, TO THEE"

SARAH FULLER FLOWER, who wrote the hymn,
"Nearer, My God to Thee," was the second daughter
of Benjamin Flower, an English Unitarian, proprietor
and editor of the Cambridge (England) *Intelligencer*.
Sarah, born 1805, composed many lyrics but had she
written nothing more than this hymn she would be
remembered.   Her sister, Eliza, who was two years
her junior, was a gifted musician.   Eliza set the verses
to music as Sarah composed them.
    At the age of twenty-nine, Sarah married an engineer
named Adams, and on the father's death, Eliza, who
was devoted to her sister, went to live with the Adams'.
    One night Sarah had a vivid dream in which she
imagined that she was standing by the mounds where
Jacob once pitched his tent in Bethel.   It was a wild
and bare sanctuary.   In her dream she saw the wander-

ing exile, Jacob, to whom Jehovah had revealed Himself in such desolate surroundings. She felt a great conviction that God was with His servants everywhere, however lonely their ways of life. She awoke, got up at once, and put down the words of this hymn. Eliza wrote a tune, which was used for some time.

The sisters were not destined to live very long. Both were victims of tuberculosis. Sarah passed away two years after the death of Eliza, at the early age of forty-three. She was buried at Harlow, Essex, England.

The hymn did not become immediately well known. Dr. Lowell Mason gave it the tune loved by all, and which is indelibly associated with the great pre-war tragedy, the Titanic disaster.

The morning after the vessel sank, all the world knew how, as the end drew near, the ship's band struck up the tune of this hymn, and passengers and crew joined in the singing. As the mighty Atlantic was about to engulf that brilliantly lighted but doomed liner with all who remained on board, the music came across the waste of waters to the survivors, secure in their life-boats—to haunt them forever:

I

Nearer, my God, to Thee,
Nearer to Thee!
E'en though it be a cross
That raiseth me:
Still all my song shall be
Nearer, my God, to Thee,
Nearer to Thee.

II

Though like the wanderer,
The sun gone down,
Darkness be over me

My rest a stone:
Yet in my dreams I'd be
    Nearer, my God, to Thee,
    Nearer to Thee.

III

There let the way appear
    Steps unto heaven:
All that Thou sendest me
    In mercy given:
Angels to beckon me,
    Nearer, my God, to Thee,
    Nearer to Thee.

IV

Then with my waking thoughts,
    Bright with Thy praise,
Out of my stony griefs
    Bethel I'll raise:
So by my woes to be
    Nearer, my God, to Thee,
    Nearer to Thee.

V

Or if on joyful wing
    Cleaving the sky,
Sun, moon, and stars forgot
    Upward, I fly.
Still all my song shall be
    Nearer, my God, to Thee,
    Nearer to Thee.

:-:-:-:

"NOW THANK WE ALL OUR GOD"

At Eilenburg, Westphalia, in the year 1586, Martin Rinkart was born. The son of a cooper, he was given a good education there and was graduated in due course from Leipzig University.

Martin was a man of amiable disposition. As a young pastor, he was much sought after to iron out the troubles of his flock. He held various pastoral offices in small towns and then in 1617 was appointed archdeacon at his birthplace, where he was to spend the rest of his time.

His life was almost entirely passed in the cloud of the Thirty Years' War. Overcrowded and stricken, the town was ravaged by pestilence. There was no other clergyman there but Rinkart. He often read forty funeral services from sun-up to sun-down.

During the occupation of the place by the Swedes he persuaded the commander not to exact more tribute than they could pay. He himself gave away almost all his means, until the resources of his family were exceedingly strained.

Martin Rinkart, pastor, poet, and musician, composed the first two verses of this devoutly moving hymn as a grace after meat. His own household sang them, deeply thankful for their food and humble dwelling.

The verses were published about 1636 in *Jesu Herzbuchlein, Leipzig.* The third verse he added as a doxology:

> Now thank we all our God,
>   With heart, and hands, and voices,
> Who wondrous things hath done,
>   In whom His world rejoices:
> Who, from our mother's arms
>   Hath blessed us on our way
> With countless gifts of love,
>   And still is ours today.
>
> Oh, may this bounteous God.
>   Through all our life be near us.
> With ever joyful hearts
>   And blessed peace to cheer us,

> *And keep us in His grace,*
> *To guide us when perplexed,*
> *And free us from all ills*
> *In this world and the next.*
>
> *All praise and thanks to God*
> *The Father now be given,*
> *The Son and Him who reigns*
> *With them in highest heaven,*
> *The one eternal God,*
> *Whom earth and heaven adore,*
> *For thus it was, is now,*
> *And shall be evermore.*

This hymn is the one chosen for all national occasions of thanksgiving.

We owe the translation to Miss Winkworth. The beautiful melody, *Nun Danket*, is from the seventeenth century Johann Cruger's famous collection, *Praxis Pictatis Melica.*

$:-:-:-:$

"NOW THE LABORER'S TASK IS O'ER"

JOHN ELLERTON was born in London in 1826. After early school days in the Isle of Man (King William's College) he graduated from Trinity College, Cambridge. During his Cambridge days he was noted for his singleness of heart and sympathetic understanding. He was of a poetical and musical temperament, a strong partisan of the Anglican faith, but neither high church nor low church—but a broadminded friend of all.

His first curacy was at Midhurst; whence he found himself at Brighton, where he wrote his first hymn (for the children). Eighty of his hymns are extant.

Afterwards at Crewe, a railway working center, he started a mechanics' institute, teaching two nights a week. He also commenced a choral class, and through his organization the first Choral Association met at Nantwich (near Chester). This became an annual event.

His health, never robust, gave way, and for twelve months he gave up all work in favor of a sea voyage. He then became Rector of White Roding, Essex, and here he stayed for the rest of his life, devoting his spare time to the compilation of his loved hymnology.

Not any hymn books of the day were complete unless Canon Ellerton had a share in their make-up. He took a guiding part in the publication of *Hymns Ancient and Modern.*

His own beautiful compositions were published in 1888, under the title of *Hymns Original and Translated.* When he was asked to take out a copyright, he refused, saying that "if they were counted worthy to contribute to Christ's praise in the congregation one ought to feel very thankful and humble."

In 1871 Canon Ellerton wrote this hymn under stress of deep sympathy, to comfort the sorrowing members of a family in his parish. It has since brought comfort to thousands.

Now the laborer's task is o'er;
Now the battle day is past;
Now upon the farther shore
Lands the voyager at last.
Father, in Thy gracious keeping
Leave we now Thy servant sleeping.

There the tears of earth are dried;
There its hidden things are clear;
There the work of life is tried
By a juster Judge than here.
Father, in Thy gracious keeping
Leave we now Thy servant sleeping.

There the sinful souls, that turn
To the cross their dying eyes,
All the love of Christ shall learn
At His feet in Paradise.
Father, in Thy gracious keeping
Leave we now Thy servant sleeping.

There no more the powers of hell
Can prevail to mar their peace;
Christ the Lord shall guard them well,
He who died for their release.
Father, in Thy gracious keeping
Leave we now Thy servant sleeping.

"Earth to earth, and dust to dust,"
Calmly now the words we say,
Leaving them to sleep in trust
Till the resurrection day.
Father, in Thy gracious keeping
Leave we now Thy servant sleeping.

:-:-:-:

"O COME, ALL YE FAITHFUL"

IT was late on Christmas Eve in the year of our
Lord, 1700. The few people abroad at that hour were
hastening to their destinations, hurrying to escape being
caught by the fog which was already beginning to hide
familiar landmarks. In the streets, men and boys
carrying torches were reaping a harvest of pennies by

escorting pedestrians and carriages on their way. Nevertheless the bells of many churches were pealing a welcome, seeming to bid those still outside to exchange the gloom of the night for the warm brightness within.

Near the Portuguese Embassy was a long string of carriages, each with a full complement of occupants, and each carriage with its resplendent footman bearing a flare, to light the way to the Embassy Chapel, where on this festive night a service, renowned for the beauty of its ritual and music drew many people of distinction. Among those invited by the Portuguese ambassador was the Duke of Leeds, "The Master of Ye Ancient Music" at the court of St. James. His grace was responsible for the concerts of their reigning majesties, William and Mary.

During the service a beautiful carol was sung (in Latin). It had been brought from France and had never before been heard in England.

The Duke was much impressed by its beauty and asked if he might have the music, declaring that "it surpassed all hymns." He called it "The Portuguese Hymn." It was:

> O come, all ye faithful,
> Joyful and triumphant,
> O come ye, O come ye to Bethlehem:
> Come and behold Him,
> Born the King of angels;
> O come, let us adore Him,
> O come, let us adore Him,
> O come, let us adore Him, Christ the Lord.
>
> God of God
> Light of Light
> Lo, He abhors not the Virgin's womb;
> Very God

Begotten, not created;
O come, let us adore Him,
O come, let us adore Him,
O come, let us adore Him, Christ the Lord.

Yea, Lord, we greet Thee,
Born this happy morning,
Jesus, to Thee be glory given;
Word of the Father,
Now in flesh appearing!
O come, let us adore Him,
O come, let us adore Him,
O come, let us adore Him, Christ the Lord.

Soon afterwards this carol was introduced at court and came to be used in every Roman Catholic Church in England.

In the year 1841 Canon Oakley translated it for his congregation at Margaret Street Chapel. It was soon widely used.

Its origin remained obscure. The only thing definitely known about it is that it was composed in France and used by the Roman Church there.

"O FOR A CLOSER WALK WITH GOD"

IN THE beautiful English county of Buckinghamshire, there nestles a little village that bears the name of Olney. Here was the home of the much loved Olney hymns composed by William Cowper and John Newton.

In the year 1769 the gentle, sensitive poet, Cowper, whose tragic life had kept him (for the most part) in retirement, was living at the parsonage, having entered

the home circle of John Newton (curate of Olney) and
the Unwin family—his faithful friends of many years,
all living together under one roof.

In the rambling garden of the parsonage was a
summer house, which was almost hidden by the surrounding trees. In this quiet retreat, Cowper spent much
of his time. The place appealed to his deep sympathy
with nature, and love of animals; so much so that he
wrote a well known poem to "the garden."

There were periods he had of lapses of memory,
when he lived entirely in the little home in the grounds.
Then it was that Mrs. Unwin's care was needed most—
to shield him from the eyes of the world.

In the winter of 1769 Mary Unwin was seriously
ill. As Cowper retired to his room on the evening of
December 9 her life was in the balance. Cowper was
much agitated by this calamity which had fallen so
suddenly upon their peaceful home life. He was desolate. Writing to a friend, he said, "She is the chief
of blessings I have met with on my journey since the
Lord was pleased to call me. . . . Her illness has been
a sharp trial to me. . . . I began to compose the verses
yesterday morning before day-break but fell asleep
at the end of the first two lines! When I awakened
again, the third and fourth were whispered to my heart
in a way which I have often experienced."

This was the hymn that was "whispered to his heart":

> O for a closer walk with God,
> A calm and heavenly frame;
> A light to shine upon the road
> That leads me to the Lamb.

What peaceful hours I once enjoyed,
How sweet their memory still!
But they have left an aching void
The world can never fill.

Return, O holy Dove, return,
Sweet messenger of rest:
I hate the sins that made Thee mourn
And drove Thee from my breast.

The dearest idol I have known,
Whate'er that idol be,
Help me to tear it from Thy throne,
And worship only Thee.

So shall my life be close with God,
Calm and serene my frame!
So purer light shall mark the road
That leads me to the Lamb.

The depth of pathos in this beautiful hymn is enhanced by the melody to which Cowper wrote the words (Ludlow). He used to hear an old cobbler hum this air and was greatly attracted to it, so wrote the hymn to suit the tune. The tune usually used now is that of "Martyrdom," composed by Hugh Wilson in 1825 and was first sung at Edinburgh, fifty-five years after Cowper's death.

"O GOD, OUR HELP IN AGES PAST"

MANY CONSIDER this hymn by Isaac Watts the finest in the English language. It was composed in 1714 during the time of national anxiety as to the succession to the throne. Queen Anne was nearing the end of her reign. She had no direct heir. Her family of eight had all died at birth. Her husband had pre-deceased her by some eight years. Her friendships had proved unhappy. She was disillusioned and lonely.

The queen had served the state well. She had been moderate, a stout-hearted Protestant, thoughtful for her people, generous and kindly, establishing out of her own pocket the renowned "Queen Anne's Bounty." She built many churches. Her people styled her "Good Queen Anne."

Comparisons of the Queen's personality with that of George of Hanover, the heir apparent, did not work to the latter's advantage, and general concern and foreboding was felt at the prospect of a man who could speak no English and knew little or nothing of English ways occupying the English throne.

Isaac Watts, a guest at the home of Sir Charles and Lady Abney, wrote this hymn to calm the nation's fears. It was published in leaflet form and distributed widely.

Some six years later, the famous organist of Westminster Abbey (Croft) composed the majestic tune (1720).

O God, our help in ages past,
Our hope for years to come,
Our shelter from the stormy blast,
And our eternal home.

Beneath the shadow of Thy throne
Thy saints have dwelt secure;
Sufficient is Thine arm alone,
And our defense is sure.

Before the hills in order stood,
Or earth received her frame,
From everlasting Thou art God
To endless years the same.

A thousand ages in Thy sight,
Are like an evening gone;
Short as the watch that ends the night,
Before the rising sun.

Time, like an ever rolling stream,
Bears all its sons away;
They fly, forgotten, as a dream
Dies at the opening day.

O God, our help in ages past,
Our hope for years to come,
Be Thou our guard while troubles last,
And our eternal home.

:-:-:-:

"O LOVE THAT WILT NOT LET ME GO"

IF YOU ARE voyaging to Glasgow and going down the Clyde you will see a long pier jutting some way out from the shore and the name "Innellan" painted in large letters on the roof. Innellan, in Argyllshire, was the home of one of Scotland's most famous sons—Dr. George Matheson—the much loved blind poet-preacher. George Matheson was born in 1842 in Glasgow, the son of a well-to-do merchant. As a boy he had much trouble with his eyes, and at eighteen he was more or less blind.

He showed remarkable gifts and was one of Glasgow's most accomplished scholars. After a brilliant undergraduate record at Edinburgh, he assisted Dr. Macduff in Glasgow, being licensed to preach, and in 1868 was appointed to the parish of Innellan.

This hymn, the author says, "was written in the Clyde-side Manse at Innellan on the evening of my sister's

wedding. I was at that time alone. It was the day
of my sister's wedding, and other members of the
family were staying overnight in Glasgow. Something
had happened to me which was known only to myself.
I was suffering from extreme mental distress and the
hymn was the fruit of pain. It was composed with
great rapidity: it seemed to me that its construction
occupied only a few minutes, and I felt myself rather
in the position of one who was being dictated to than
an original artist. It was the quickest piece of work
I have ever done. I am sure that the whole hymn was
completed in five minutes, neither did I ever correct
or retouch any part of it."

O Love that wilt not let me go,
  I rest my weary soul in Thee:
I give Thee back the life I owe,
That in Thine ocean depths its flow
  May richer, fuller be.

O Light that followest all my way,
  I yield my flickering torch to Thee:
My heart restores its borrowed ray,
That in Thy sunshine's blaze its day
  May brighter, fairer be.

O joy that seekest me through pain,
  I cannot close my heart to Thee:
I trace the Rainbow through the rain,
And feel the promise is not vain
  That morn shall tearless be.

O Cross that liftest up my head,
  I dare not ask to fly from thee:
I lay in dust life's glory dead,
And from the ground there blossoms red
  Life that shall endless be.

This beautiful and fervent hymn took Scotland by storm when it was written over seventy years ago.

The *Scottish Hymnal* wished to have it in their new publication in 1885. Dr. Peace, of Arran, was asked to write a suitable tune.

Dr. Peace says, "After reading it over carefully I wrote the music straight off and I may say that the ink of the first note was hardly dry when I had finished the tune."

:-:-:-:

"ONWARD, CHRISTIAN SOLDIERS"

WHEN THE Rev. Sabine Baring-Gould was rector of Hornbury Bridge, Yorkshire, he had a scattered parish and a very large Sunday school. The school building was some little way from the church. It was the custom on festivals (Whit-Monday is a great day for festivals in Yorkshire) for the Sunday school to march to the church in procession before going to the annual tea. A larger festival than usual was planned for Whit-Monday, 1865. Starting from Hornbury Bridge, a procession was to go from village to village, returning by a circular route for the service at Hornbury Church before the big fete.

Mr. Baring-Gould wanted the children to sing as they marched from one parish to another, but he says, "I couldn't think of anything suitable, so I resolved that I would write something myself. I sat up all night, writing in great haste. I was too engrossed to give up. On Sunday morning 'Onward, Christian Soldiers' was the result." He soon had some leaflets printed and the school was taught to sing it to "Gauntlets" tune.

It was a warm and bright day in May. The author's joy was unbounded on hearing the evident pleasure of the young people singing, and the success of the marching words.

In later years the great popularity of this processional hymn is in part due to his friend Sullivan, who gave to it the stirring tune so well known and loved throughout the English-speaking world.

Mr. Baring-Gould died in 1924 at the age of ninety years. He is chiefly famous as the author of this hymn. He also wrote the exquisite Easter hymn, "On the Resurrection Morning," and "Now the Day is Over."

Onward, Christian soldiers
Marching as to war,
With the cross of Jesus
Going on before.
Christ the Royal Master,
Leads against the foe,
Forward into battle
See His banners go.
Onward, Christian soldiers,
Marching as to war
With the cross of Jesus
Going on before.

At the sign of triumph,
Satan's host doth flee;
On then, Christian soldiers,
On to victory!
Hell's foundations quiver
At the shout of praise;
Brothers, lift your voices,
Loud your anthems raise.
Chorus

Like a mighty army,
Moves the church of God,
Brothers, we are treading
Where the saints have trod.
We are not divided,
All one body we,
One in hope and doctrine,
One in charity.

Chorus

Crowns and thrones may perish,
Kingdoms rise and wane;
But the church of Jesus
Constant will remain;
Gates of hell can never
'Gainst that church prevail;
We have Christ's own promise,
And that cannot fail.

Chorus

:-:-:-:

"O PERFECT LOVE"

WHEN Dorothy Frances Blomfield was a little girl,
her father was the rector of a popular church in the
Strand, bearing the quaint name of St. Andrew's-Under-
Shaft. (In olden days a maypole — or shaft, over-
shadowed this spot, and Chaucer refers to it in one of
his poems.) Her grandfather was bishop of London
and Chester.

On her marriage to the Rev. Archer Gurney, she
entered into a poetical family, which suited her literary
temperament. Her husband's father was a writer of
hymns and gave Dorothy sympathetic encouragement
in her work. Her marriage was a happy one.

Later, she published a book of poems, and one of the verses is quoted the world over:

> *The kiss of the sun for pardon*
> *The song of the birds for mirth;*
> *One is nearer God's heart in a garden*
> *Than anywhere else on earth.*

When she was twenty-five years of age, she was staying at a little place in the lake district of England named Pull Wyke, Windermere. She had arrived there for her sister's wedding which was to take place shortly. In the peace of the quiet Sunday evening, she was thinking thoughtfully of the marriage, and of the happiness of the young pair, and seizing a pencil, she wrote down this beautiful hymn, to be sung at the marriage service. She relates how "it only took fifteen minutes to write." It was sung to the tune of another hymn, which Dr. Dykes had composed.

> *O perfect Love, all human thought transcending,*
> *Lowly we kneel in prayer before Thy throne,*
> *That theirs may be the love which knows no ending,*
> *Whom Thou forevermore dost join in one.*
>
> *O perfect Life, be Thou their full assurance*
> *Of tender charity and stedfast faith,*
> *Of patient hope, and quiet, brave endurance,*
> *With childlike trust that fears no pain nor death.*
>
> *Grant them the joy which brightens earthly sorrow,*
> *Grant them the peace which calms all earthly strife;*
> *And to life's day the glorious unknown morrow*
> *That dawns upon eternal love and life.*

At the marriage (six years afterwards) of the Duke and Duchess of Fife (daughter of King Edward VII)

Sir Joseph Barnaby composed an anthem for the occasion, which he afterwards adapted to this popular marriage hymn. It soon became the fashion at all social weddings, and is universally loved.

:-:-:-:

"OUR BLEST REDEEMER"

IN 1765, Pierre Auber swiftly gathered up his portable possessions and with his family fled to England. Normandy was no place for Huguenots after the revocation of the Edict of Nantes. About eighty years or so later, his grandson, James Auber, was living in London and celebrating the birth of his second daughter, Harriet.

A few years afterwards they found themselves in a large country house containing a beautiful garden in the village of Hoddesdon, Huntingdonshire. There Harriet grew up into an attractive and charming girl, whose gentle spirit filled the home.

She wrote lyrics as well as prose, some of which were published locally. Much she would not show even to her parents, but her writings were sought by her friends.

One day in May, 1809, she was walking in the garden, engrossed in her personal affairs. She seemed to have a premonition that all was not well, and as she thought, she twirled her engagement ring round her finger, pressing it to her lips and wondering if she would ever see her lover back from the Peninsular. Before his departure he had asked her to care for his motherless son. While thinking over these things, she

came upon the boy trying to help a dove that had hurt
its wing. Together they stroked and calmed the frightened bird, and when it alighted on her shoulder,
friendly and tame, she felt that the dove had been a
comforter to her own heart.

Dreamily she went up to her room and sat on the
deep seat by the casement window. On a sudden inspiration she wanted to write down what was in her
mind, but remembered that she had no paper. Her
father was returning from London the next day with it.
Write she must; so taking off her diamond ring, she
traced on the window-pane:

> *Our blest Redeemer, ere He breathed*
> *His tender last farewell,*
> *A Guide, a Comforter, bequeathed*
> *With us to dwell.*
>
> *He came sweet influence to impart,*
> *A gracious willing guest,*
> *While He can find one humble heart*
> *Wherein to rest.*
>
> *And every virtue we possess,*
> *And every conquest won*
> *And every thought of holiness*
> *Are His alone.*
>
> *Spirit of purity and grace,*
> *Our weakness, pitying, see,*
> *O make our hearts Thy dwelling-place*
> *And worthier Thee.*

Harriet was then thirty-five. Her fiance was killed
at Waterloo. The little boy grew to manhood, always
the devoted attendant of the gentle lady, who, with her

literary friend, Miss Mary MacKenzie, mellowed the place, until her death at the age of eighty-nine.

The pane was not removed during their lifetime and was still there some years after her death. It then disappeared mysteriously. But the later occupants of the house were never alarmed at a gentle Presence which seemed to hover in the little casement-room—sitting by the window—waiting!

"PEACE, PERFECT PEACE"

THERE IS a quaint house in Harrogate (Yorkshire) that faces the Stray (Street). In the summer of 1875 a family came there from London for a holiday. It was the family of Edward Henry Bickersteth, who was then about fifty. His son related the following story:

"On a Sunday morning in August the Vicar of Harrogate, Canon Gibbon, happened to preach from the text, 'Thou wilt keep him in perfect peace whose mind is stayed on Thee,' and alluded to the fact that in the Hebrew the words are 'Peace, peace' twice repeated, and happily translated in the 1611 translation by the phrase 'Perfect peace.'

"His sermon set my father's mind working on the subject. He always found it easiest to express in verse whatever subject was uppermost in his mind, and so when on the afternoon of that Sunday he visited an aged and dying relative (Archdeacon Hill of Liverpool) and found him somewhat troubled in mind, it was natural to him to express in verse the spiritual comfort which he desired to convey.

"Taking up a sheet of paper, he then and there wrote down the hymn just exactly as it stands, and read it to the dying man. I was with my father at the time, being home from school for the summer holidays, and I well recollect his coming in to tea, a meal which we always had with him on Sunday afternoons, and saying, 'Children, I have written you a hymn,' and reading us, 'Peace, Perfect Peace,' in which from the moment he wrote it, he never made any alteration."

Peace, perfect peace, in this dark world of sin,
The blood of Jesus whispers peace within.

Peace, perfect peace, with sorrows surging round?
On Jesus' bosom naught but calm is found.

Peace, perfect peace, with loved ones far away?
In Jesus' keeping we are safe and they.

Peace, perfect peace, our future all unknown?
Jesus we know, and He is on the throne.

Peace, perfect peace, death shadowing us and ours?
Jesus has vanquished death and all its powers.

It is enough! Earth's struggles soon shall cease,
And Jesus calls us to Heaven's perfect peace.

Edward Bickersteth, D.D., was born in London, 1825, graduating from Trinity College, Cambridge. In 1885 he became the Bishop of Exeter in succession to Dr. Temple. He was a poet by nature, and published several volumes, both of verse and prose, but this hymn is the shining star of all his works.

The tune was composed by a young man named Caldbeck. He was training to be a missionary but on account of ill health was unsuitable. On one occasion, having shut himself into his room for quiet, he issued forth with this melody. It was sent to Dr. Bickersteth and became at once inseparably associated with the words.

:-:-:-:

"ROCK OF AGES"

THE AUTHOR of "Rock of Ages," Augustus Montague Toplady, was born in 1740. His father, Major Toplady, was killed in the War in Spain, leaving the son, whom he had never seen, to the care of a devoted mother. The boy, after spending some time at Westminster School, went to live in Ireland where he attended Trinity College, Dublin.

When holidaying with his mother one vacation he overheard some people singing in a barn near by. Investigating, he saw some simple country folk holding a prayer-meeting. They were singing a hymn. Out of curiosity he stayed and heard an uneducated man speak, taking for his text Eph. 2:13: "Ye who sometimes were far off, are made nigh by the blood of Christ." Toplady readily admitted afterwards that he was a changed man from that time. He wrote, "Strange that I should meet God in an obscure part of Ireland, midst a handful of people met together in a barn, and by the ministry of one who could scarcely spell his own name. Surely it was the Lord's doing and it was marvelous. It cannot be of man—it is of God."

Later he became curate-in-charge of the parish of

Blagdon, near the Mendip range in the West country, about eight miles from Wells. Toplady was very fond of taking long walks down the lanes of this beautiful part of England and on one occasion while walking in the rocky glen of Barrington Combe he was overtaken by a severe thunderstorm. Looking round for a refuge he could find nothing suitable in sight but a great split down the granite rock of the bank near him. He climbed into the fissure and he was completely sheltered. As he watched the vivid lightning and heard the roar of the thunder, he formed in his mind the words of this hymn:

> *Rock of Ages, cleft for me,*
> *Let me hide myself in Thee;*
> *Let the water and the blood*
> *From Thy riven side which flowed*
> *Be of sin the double cure,*
> *Cleanse me from its guilt and power.*
>
> *Not the labors of my hands,*
> *Can fulfil Thy law's demands;*
> *Could my zeal no respite know,*
> *Could my tears for ever flow,*
> *All for sin could not atone,*
> *Thou must save, and Thou alone.*
>
> *Nothing in my hand I bring;*
> *Simply to Thy cross I cling;*
> *Naked, come to Thee for dress,*
> *Helpless, look to Thee for grace,*
> *Foul I to the fountain fly,*
> *Wash me, Savior, or I die.*
>
> *While I draw this fleeting breath,*
> *When mine eyelids close in death,*
> *When I rise to worlds unknown,*
> *See Thee on Thy judgment throne,*
> *Rock of Ages, cleft for me,*
> *Let me hide myself in Thee.*

On reaching his home he wrote down the verses.
This hymn was first published in 1775. Toplady died
of tuberculosis three years afterwards at the early age
of thirty-eight years but the hymn he wrote will live
as long as the Christian church. This story is well
known in the district, and the writer heard it from the
lips of the village people.

:-:-:-:

"SAFE IN THE ARMS OF JESUS"

FANNY CROSBY has brought comfort to millions of
people. Her hymns have reached all lands and climes.
This blind poetess, from whose seeming darkness a beam
of light swept around the world, was born at Putnam
County, New York, in 1820. She was deeply sensitive,
as many blind people are, showing early a keen desire
for knowledge. She learned several of the Gospels
off by heart. She began to write verse when she was
eight years old. At fifteen, she was sent to a school
for the blind in New York City.

William Cullen Bryant visited the school one day
and gave Fanny much encouragement for some verses
of hers he had chanced to read. She said afterwards,
"He never knew how much he did by those few words."
In 1858 she was married to Mr. Alexander Van Alstyne,
a teacher in the school for the blind.

Her greatest hymn came to be written in a very
unusual manner. One day she had a visit from her
friend, Dr. W. H. Doane, himself a composer of some
merit. His visit had to be short as he had a special
engagement that evening. He said, "Fanny, I'm in

somewhat of a hurry but I wonder if you could write
me some words for this music?" He went over to the
piano and played the tune. He then played it again,
slowly. She took pencil and paper, as he played it
slowly once more, and she wrote:

> Safe in the arms of Jesus,
>   Safe on His gentle breast,
> There by His love o'ershaded
>   Sweetly my soul shall rest.
> Hark! 'tis the voice of angels,
>   Borne in a song to me.
> Over the fields of glory,
>   Over the crystal sea.

>> Safe in the arms of Jesus,
>>   Safe on His gentle breast,
>> There by His love o'ershaded,
>>   Sweetly my soul shall rest.

> Safe in the arms of Jesus,
>   Safe from corroding care,
> Safe from the world's temptation,
>   Sin cannot harm me there;
> Free from the blight of sorrow,
>   Free from my doubts and fears,
> Only a few more trials
>   Only a few more tears.
>>   Safe in the arms of Jesus, etc.

> Jesus my heart's dear refuge,
>   Jesus has died for me
> Firm on the rock of ages
>   Ever my trust shall be;
> Here let me wait with patience
>   Wait till the night is o'er,
> Wait till I see the morning
>   Break on the golden shore.
>>   Safe in the arms of Jesus, etc.

Dr. Doane was very much touched by the simple and sweet words Fanny had written, and told her so. She said, "They seemed to come to me without any effort." He took them away with him and had them published.

Ira D. Sankey made this hymn famous the world over when he sang it into the people's hearts, and it was not forgotten.

:-:-:-:

"SHALL WE GATHER AT THE RIVER?"

THE Rev. Robert Lowry, D.D., was born in Philadelphia, Pa., in 1826. Early in life he felt himself called to the work of the church. He entered the ministry of the Baptist denomination. At one time he held the Chair of Rhetoric at Lewisburg.

Dr. Lowry had the Sunday school work much at heart, and entered, with interest, into the publication of suitable books for the young. He had considerable musical ability and set most of his hymns to tunes which caught the public fancy. This hymn is not considered his masterpiece, but it is the one by which his name became widely known. His friend, Ira D. Sankey, told how this hymn came to be written:

"On a sultry afternoon in July, 1864, Dr. Lowry was sitting at his table in Elliot Place, Brooklyn, where the words of this hymn, 'Shall We Gather at the River' came to him. An epidemic was raging through the city at the time, and he had been pondering the question, 'Why do hymn-writers say so much about the river of death and so little about the pure river of the water of

life?' It was a sad time for many. All around friends
and acquaintances were passing away to the spirit-land.
The question began to arise in the heart with unusual
emphasis, 'Shall we meet at the river of life?' He
hastily recorded the words. 'Seating myself at the
parlor organ,' he said, 'simply to give vent to the
pent-up emotions of the heart, came the words as if
by inspiration:' "

> *Shall we gather at the river,*
> *Where bright angel feet have trod;*
> *With its crystal tide forever*
> *Flowing from the Throne of God?*

> *Yes, we will gather at the river,*
> *The beautiful, the beautiful river;*
> *Gather with the saints at the river,*
> *That flows from the Throne of God.*

> *On the margin of the river,*
> *Guided by our Shepherd King,*
> *We will walk and worship ever,*
> *His dear footsteps following.*
>   Chorus

> *There, beside the tranquil river,*
> *Mirror of the Savior's face,*
> *Happy hearts no more to sever,*
> *Sing of glory and of grace.*
>   Chorus

> *Ere we reach the shining river,*
> *Lay we every burden down;*
> *Jesus, here from sin deliver*
> *Those whom there Thy grace will crown.*
>   Chorus

This hymn was published in many hymnals all over the world and of all denominations. Sankey often sang it and made it popular. When Dr. Lowry was visiting London in 1880, on the occasion of the Sunday School Workers meeting for the Raikes Centenary, he was given a great ovation when introduced as the author of this hymn.

:-:-:-:

"SOMETIME WE'LL UNDERSTAND"

At Spurgeon's Tabernacle, London, in 1892, the noted evangelist, Moody, was holding a mission. Great interest in these gatherings was shown by the social world of Mayfair, with the poor of the slums. Everywhere the mission was the topic of conversation. Queen Victoria was graciously pleased to hear of the good work and enjoyed listening to the simple gospel hymns. . . . These same gospel hymns were sermons in themselves, their simple words with tender appeal seldom failing to reach the hearts of their hearers.

It was the custom at this mission for people to send in "requests" for certain hymns to be sung some particular evening. One day, a request was received from Princess May (Queen Mary) whose fiance, the Duke of Clarence (King George V's brother) had died some little time previously. The Duchess of Teck and her daughter, Princess May, were in the audience that evening, and listened with rapt attention while the composer (J. McGranahan) sang the understanding words of this hymn:

Not now, but in the coming years—
It may be in the better land—
We'll read the meaning of our tears,
And there, sometime, we'll understand.

Then trust in God through all Thy days:
Fear not, for He doth hold Thy hand:
Though dark thy way, still sing and praise;
Sometime, sometime we'll understand.

We'll catch the broken threads again,
That snapped while they were in our hand:
Heaven will the mysteries explain,
And then, ah, then, we'll understand.

We'll know why clouds instead of sun
O'ershadowed all our promised land:
Why song has ceased when scarce begun;
'Tis then, sometime, we'll understand.

Why what we long for most of all
Eludes so oft our eager hand.
Why hopes are crushed, and castles fall
Up there, sometime, we'll understand.

God knows the way, He holds the key,
He guides us with unerring hand;
Sometime with tearless eyes we'll see;
Yes, there, up there, we'll understand.

These simple words were received in palace and cottage alike, leaving a fragrance with the passing years, to echo in a new generation. Mr. J. McGranahan died at Kinsman, Ohio, at the age of sixty-seven.

"TAKE MY LIFE AND LET IT BE"

Two YEARS ago there was celebrated the centenary of the birth of Frances Ridley Havergal. At the time her father was the rector of Astley, Worcestershire. Frances was the youngest child and was made much of. In adolescence her health gave some slight cause for anxiety. Not allowed to go to school, she acquired an education casually, and when she grew older she traveled.

Frances loved poetry. Composition of verses came easily to her, and she exercised her gift by putting the daily round in rhyme. Always inclined to the spiritual, as her years increased so did her devotion to good works. Early in life she called Christ her "Master" and proclaimed that she was ready for His service at any time.

How this hymn came to be written has often been told. In February, 1874, Frances went on a visit to London to stay with intimate friends. But their ways were not quite her ways. They were a large family, and each in turn confided his hopes and fears to her sympathetic ear. Her visit was not to be a long one, and as the time for her departure drew near, she prayed that she might be allowed to help them all.

The night before she was leaving, first one, then the others following, came to her room, and went away comforted. Filled with happiness that her prayers were answered she said that unable to sleep, these little couplets formed in her heart, and going to her desk she wrote down the beautiful words:

> Take my life, and let it be
> Consecrated, Lord, to Thee:
> Take my moments and my days,
> Let them flow in ceaseless praise.

Take my hands, and let them move
At the impulse of Thy love:
Take my feet, and let them be
Filled with messages from Thee.

Take my silver and my gold,
Not a mite would I withhold:
Take my intellect, and use
Every power as Thou shalt choose.

Take my will, and make it Thine:
It shall be no longer mine:
Take my heart, it is Thine own:
It shall be Thy royal throne.

Take my love, my Lord, I pour
At Thy feet its treasure store:
Take myself, and I will be,
Ever, only, all for Thee.

:-:-:-:

"THE DAY OF RESURRECTION"

IN THE YEAR 720 A.D. there lived in Damascus a young Greek scholar whose name was John. As a child he had shown a desire for learning. He dwelt with his adopted brother Cosmas, an Italian monk, who had an important office of state and was termed a "Methodist."

In this home of learning, John's ready mind quickly assimilated both the new and ancient lore. He became the greatest poet of the century and an earnest writer on the life of our blessed Lord. After some years of acclamation as a person of importance, he decided to give away all he possessed and retire to live with

Cosmas at the Monastery of St. Sabas (between Jerusalem and the Dead Sea) there to devote his life to writing manuscripts and canons (laws) for the Medieval Church. This hymn is part of a canon written for Christian worship Easter, 750 A.D., as meaningful today as then.

This legacy of St. John of Damascus of twelve hundred years ago is:

The day of Resurrection!
Earth, tell it out abroad;
The Passover of gladness,
The Passover of God!
From death to life eternal,
From earth unto the sky,
Our God hath brought us over
With hymns of victory.

Our hearts be pure from evil,
That we may see aright,
The Lord in rays eternal
Of resurrection light;
And, listening to His accents,
May hear so calm and plain
His own "All Hail" and hearing
May raise the victor strain.

The great translator, Dr. Neale, tells in his own words how Easter was kept!

"The scene is at Athens (Easter Eve). As midnight approaches, the archbishop with his priests, accompanied by the King and Queen, left the church and stationed themselves on the platform, which had been raised considerably from the ground, so that they were distinctly seen by the people. Everyone now remained in breathless expectation holding their unlighted tapers in readiness when the glad moment should arrive, while the priests still continued murmuring their melancholy chant in a low half-whisper."

Suddenly a single report of a cannon announced that twelve o'clock had struck and that Easter Day had begun; then the old archbishop, elevating the cross, exclaimed in a loud, exulting tone, "Christos Anesti," "Christ is Risen," "Christ is Risen." At the same moment the oppressive darkness was succeeded by a blaze of light from thousands of tapers which, communicating one from another, seemed to send streams of fire in all directions, rendering the minutest objects distinctly visible and casting the most vivid glow on the expressive faces of the rejoicing crowd; bands of music struck up their gayest strains; the roll of drums through the town, and further on the pealing of the cannon, announced far and near these "glad tidings of great joy." While from hill and plain, from sea-shore and the far olive grove, rocket after rocket ascending to the clear sky answered back with their mute eloquence that Christ is risen indeed, and told of other tongues that were repeating those blessed words and other hearts that leaped for joy! Everywhere men clasped each others hands, and congratulated one another, and embraced with countenances beaming with delight as though to each one separately some wonderful happiness had been proclaimed." And so:

> Now let the heavens be joyful,
>   Let earth her song begin,
> Let all the world keep triumph,
>   And all that is therein:
> In grateful exultation
>   Their notes let all things blend,
> For Christ the Lord hath risen,
> Our Joy that hath no end.

"THE SANDS OF TIME ARE SINKING"

In 1824 there lived in the little Scottish town of
Leith, David Ross Cundell, M.D., who, having served
in the army at Waterloo as surgeon, was living in retirement and was the proud father of an only child,
a newborn daughter. But the doctor was not to live
much longer. When the little girl, Ann, was three
years old her father died. The widow went to Edinburgh to live and as Ann grew up she showed remarkable talent in the world of music and in languages.
The New Testament in Greek was familiar to her. As
a child she was accustomed to attend the Episcopalian
Church but turned to the Presbyterian faith and became
one of its staunch supporters.

Scotland regarded her as their Christine Possett.

In 1874 she married the Rev. William Cousin, who
was at that time the minister of Chelsea Presbyterian
Church, London. Soon after the marriage they moved
to Irvine, where her husband had been appointed
minister of the Free Kirk. While living at the Manse,
Ann Cousin, who had previously written verse anony-
mously, published several poems. This hymn, written
at that time, was inspired after reading a book on the
Scottish martyr, Samuel Rutherford, whose dying words
were:

"God dwelleth in Emmanuel's Land."

Ann Cousin tells how her mother composed the hymn
verse by verse as she sewed, and afterwards wove the
verses together.

In the hymn-books only five verses are used:

The sands of time are sinking,
  The dawn of heaven breaks,
The summer morn I've longed for,
  The fair sweet morn awakes.
Dark, dark hath been the midnight,
  But dayspring is at hand,
And glory, glory dwelleth
  In Emmanuel's Land.

O Christ, He is the fountain,
  The deep sweet well of love;
The streams on earth I've tasted
  More deep I'll drink above;
There, to an ocean fulness,
  His mercy doth expand,
And glory, glory dwelleth
  In Emmanuel's Land.

With mercy and with judgment
  My web of time He wove;
And aye the dews of sorrow
  Were lustered with His love.
I'll bless the hand that guided
  I'll bless the hand that planned,
When throned where glory dwelleth
  In Emmanuel's Land.

I'll fall asleep in Jesus,
  Filled with His likeness rise
To live and to adore Him,
  To see Him with these eyes.
The King of kings in Zion
  My presence doth command,
Where glory, glory dwelleth
  In Emmanuel's Land.

I've wrestled on towards heaven,
  'Gainst storm and wind and tide,
Lord, grant Thy weary traveler
  To lean on Thee as guide.

And 'mid the shades of evening,
While sinks life's lingering sand,
To hail the glory dawning,
In Emmanuel's Land.

This hymn was a favorite of C. H. Spurgeon, who chose it the last time he held a service in Mentone, January, 1892. Mrs. Cousin lived to see her famous poem sung around the world. She died in Edinburgh at the age of eighty-two.

:-:-:-:

"THERE IS A GREEN HILL FAR AWAY"

THE gifted author of this hymn was Frances Humphries, born in 1823, the second daughter of Major Humphries, of Milton County, Tyrone, Ireland. A woman of great charm of manner, she married the Rev. Dr. Alexander, Bishop of Derry and Raphoe. Mrs. Alexander always felt drawn to young people and devoted herself to them. At the time in which she lived schools were not as they are today. Many people from poor surroundings were illiterate. Ignorance and poverty were widespread. Education was expensive and not for poor folk. Sunday schools were dull, and there were very few hymns children could understand.

Miss Humphries determined to teach the gospel through hymns and poetry. She began to write for her Sunday school simple hymns in narrative form, easily remembered. The children loved her, and they learned the hymns by heart.

In the summer of 1848 (Miss Humphries was married in 1850) she wrote for them the lovely words:

> *All things bright and beautiful,*
> *All creatures great and small,*
> *All things wise and wonderful,*
> *The Lord God made them all.*

Followed by the hymn that begins:

> *We are but little children weak,*
> *Nor born in any high estate;*
> *What can we do for Jesus' sake*
> *Who is so high, and good, and great?*

And then for Christmas:

> *Once in Royal David's city*
> *Stood a lowly cattle-shed,*
> *Where a mother laid her baby*
> *In a manger for His bed;*
> *Mary was that mother mild,*
> *Jesus Christ her little child.*

Mrs. Alexander wrote many other hymns for children. Not the least beautiful are the sad lines that run:

> *There is a green hill far away,*
> *Outside a city wall,*
> *Where the dear Lord was crucified,*
> *Who died to save us all.*

> *We may not know, we cannot tell*
> *What pains He had to bear,*
> *But we believe it was for us*
> *He hung and suffered there.*

> *He died that we might be forgiven*
> *He died to make us good,*
> *That we might go at last to heaven,*
> *Saved by His precious blood.*

There was no other good enough
To pay the price of sin,
He only could unlock the gate
Of heaven, and let us in.

O dearly, dearly has He loved,
And we must love Him, too,
And trust in His redeeming blood,
And try His works to do.

The singing of this hymn has touched the heart of many a child. Queen Victoria herself wept over it when it was sung by the late Dame Clara Butt.

:-:-:-:

"THERE IS A LAND OF PURE DELIGHT"

Isaac Watts, the eldest of nine children, was born in Southampton, July 24, 1674. His taste for verse showed itself in his childhood. His father, Dr. Watts, was a Nonconformist minister, who, deeply revered by his congregation, was twice sent to prison for his religious convictions.

Isaac received a classical education at the grammar school, Southampton. He showed such promise of scholarship that he was twice offered free education to fit him for ordination in the Church of England, an offer that was refused for him by his father. He attended a Nonconformist Academy at Stoke Newington, for four years, and at the age of twenty left the place and spent the next two years at home.

During this time he wrote a number of hymns that were sung from Mss. in the Southampton Chapel. The first hymn he composed was "Behold the Glories of the Lamb," which brought requests for more work.

The Isle of Wight had a great fascination for him. He would spend much time walking over that beautiful countryside. On one of these occasions, while gazing at the enchanting view of the mainland, the suggestion of this exquisite hymn came to him. Envisioning the beautiful green of the New Forest across on the other side, he scribbled on a piece of paper:

> *There is a land of pure delight*
> *Where saints immortal reign:*
> *Infinite day excludes the night,*
> *And pleasures banish pain.*
>
> *There everlasting spring abides,*
> *And never withering flowers:*
> *Death, like a narrow sea, divides*
> *This heavenly land of ours.*
>
> *Sweet fields beyond the swelling flood*
> *Stand dressed in living green:*
> *So to the Jews old Canaan stood,*
> *While Jordan rolled between.*
>
> *But timorous mortals start and shrink*
> *To cross the narrow sea,*
> *And linger shivering on the brink,*
> *And fear to launch away.*
>
> *O could we make our hearts remove*
> *These gloomy doubts that rise,*
> *And see the Canaan that we love*
> *With unbeclouded eyes!*
>
> *Could we but climb where Moses stood,*
> *And view the landscape o'er:*
> *Not Jordan's stream, nor death's cold flood,*
> *Should fright us from the shore.*

Isaac Watts was twenty-one when he wrote this. At twenty-two he became tutor to the son of an eminent Puritan, Sir John Hartopp. At twenty-four he preached his first sermon as pastor of the Independent Congregation, Mark Lane (he had as a member of his congregation, Mrs. Bendish, Cromwell's granddaughter). His health, never robust, was attacked by a fever in 1712. Upon recovery from this illness he was a guest of Sir Thomas Abdney. With this family he stayed for the rest of his suffering life, a confirmed invalid. Nevertheless he lived out the allotted span of three score years and ten, dying in 1748, twenty years after the University of Edinburgh had bestowed its highest honor upon him.

He was buried in the Puritan resting-place at Bunhill Fields, London.

:-:-:-:

"THERE'S A FRIEND FOR LITTLE CHILDREN"

ALBERT MIDLANE, born 1825, at Newport, Isle of Wight, was the happy author of what is perhaps the most famous children's hymn. He was a posthumous son, which made life a little harder for him in his early years. He began to work as a young lad and was apprenticed to an iron-monger. In his spare time he wrote poetry, which he was too shy to show.

His people belonged to a sect called the "Strict Brethren." Albert went to the Sunday school and found in the teacher a kind and encouraging friend who did much to shape his early life. He found here everything to make his life happy and to inspire. The Sunday school was his greatest pleasure, first as pupil, then as teacher. All his life he lived and worked in the Isle of Wight.

One day in February, 1859, while occupied in his store, he scribbled on a piece of paper some words that came to him. That evening, when all was quiet, he sat down to write. He was so engrossed in his work that morning stole into the windows, but at any cost he meant to finish the verse. When his wife came to search for him she found him asleep, with his head resting on this now famous hymn. He had written for posterity:

> There's a Friend for little children
>   Above the bright blue sky,
> A Friend who never changes,
>   Whose love will never die;
> Our earthly friends may fail us,
>   And change with changing years,
> This Friend is always worthy
>   Of that dear Name he bears.
>
> There's a rest for little children
>   Above the bright blue sky,
> Who love the blessed Savior,
>   And to the Father cry;
> A rest from every turmoil,
>   From sin and sorrow free;
> Where every little pilgrim
>   Shall rest eternally.
>
> There's a home for little children
>   Above the bright blue sky,
> Where Jesus reigns in glory,
>   A home of peace and joy;
> No home on earth is like it,
>   Nor can with it compare,
> For everyone is happy,
>   Nor could be happier there.

There's a song for little children
Above the bright blue sky;
A song that will not weary
Though sung continually;
A song which even angels
Can never, never sing,
They know not Christ as Savior,
But worship Him as King.

There's a robe for little children
Above the bright blue sky;
And a harp of sweetest music,
And a palm of victory.
All, all above is treasured,
And found in Christ alone;
Lord, grant Thy little children
To know Thee as their own.

Dr. Robert Parker, meeting him once, said, "I would rather have written that hymn than preach the most eloquent sermon—your congregation is the whole world! Years passed, taking with them many of the young people (now grown up) to all parts of the world. Time had also made a difference to Albert Midlane. His once prosperous business had fallen on evil days. Things were bad and he feared that he would lose all he had worked for. But he kept his faith. When things were at their lowest ebb, a miracle happened!

The *Post* brought him a letter containing a check, a gift from all the Sunday school children throughout England to help their friend begin anew! The congregation in St. Paul's Cathedral, that had gathered to commemorate the jubilee of this famous hymn, heard three thousand children sing these sweet words to the joyful tune of Sir John Stainer. Nor could they forget that other scene in 1909, when a small company gathered at Carisbrooke Cemetery and laid this noble man to his rest, with the melodious strains of children's voices singing his immortal hymn.

:-:-:-:

"THERE WERE NINETY AND NINE"

IN 1832, Andrew Clephane, with his wife and three young daughters, moved from their home in Edinburgh to the little town of Melrose (made famous to the world by Sir Walter Scott in *The Abbot* and *The Monastery*). Their father had become sheriff of Fife. The little girls were devoted to each other and remained so all their lives. After their father's death they moved with their mother to East Lothian, but soon returned to Melrose, the home they knew so well.

One of them, Elizabeth, a delicate girl, was of a retiring nature. She wrote poetry, also several hymns, which were published in a paper called *The Family Treasury* under the caption, "Breathings on the Border." She was known as "Sunshine" in the homes of the poor.

Generous to a fault, the sisters devoted all their surplus funds to good works, so much so that at the end of each year they would send for the treasurer of their church (Free Kirk) and write a check to cover any deficit. There were times when they had to sacrifice their personal comfort to do so.

When Elizabeth was thirty-six she wrote the following hymn, which was published in a child's magazine called *The Children's Hour*. She died the next year.

Some five years after her death Sankey and Moody were in the train going from Glasgow to Edinburgh. As Sankey idly turned over the pages of a magazine he came across Elizabeth's poem and tried to interest Moody, but without result. However, he cut it out and put it into his pocket.

At the meeting that afternoon in Edinburgh, the subject had been "The Good Shepherd." Finishing his address, he turned to Sankey and asked him to sing some fitting solo. Sankey was in a quandary. He at once thought of the poem in his pocket! So, going to the organ, he put the print in front of him and prayed for understanding. He relates "how he struck the chord of A flat" and began to sing.

Note by note the tune was given, which remains unchanged to this day. "I knew that my song had reached the hearts of the audience," wrote Mr. Sankey afterwards. "Mr. Moody was in tears—and so was I—at the end of the hymn."

During their mission, Moody and Sankey visited Melrose. The Misses Clephane were in the audience. One may imagine the sisters' surprise upon hearing the hymn sung—their first knowledge that the world had made it its own.

> There were ninety and nine that safely lay
>   In the shelter of the fold:
> But one was out on the hills away,
>   Far off from the gates of gold.
> Away on the mountains wild and bare,
> Away from the tender Shepherd's care.
>
> "Lord, Thou hast here Thy ninety and nine,
>   Are they not enough for Thee?"
> But the Shepherd made answer: "This of mine

Has wandered away from Me:
And although the road be rough and steep,
I go to the desert to find my sheep."

But none of the ransomed ever knew
   How deep were the waters crossed;
*Nor how dark was the night that the Lord **passed***
      through
   Ere He found His sheep that was lost.
Out in the desert, He heard the cry,
Sick, and helpless, and ready to die.

But all through the mountains thunder-riven
   And up from the rocky steep,
There arose a glad cry to the gates of heaven,
   "Rejoice, I have found My sheep."
And the angels echoed around the throne,
Rejoice, for the Lord brings back His own.

:-:-:-:

"THINE FOREVER"

IN THE parish church of Overton, Flintshire, there
is a memorial tablet that reads simply:

MARY FOWLER MAUDE
BORN 1819.   DIED 1913.
THINE FOREVER!   OH, HOW BLEST
THEY WHO FIND IN THEE THEIR REST.

It is to the authoress of this beautiful hymn.

Mary Fowler Hooper was born in London. She was
highly educated and had remarkable literary gifts.
Fond of writing Eastern stories and description, she had
several books published early in life. She was versatile
and familiar with many branches of knowledge.

At the age of twenty-two she married the Rev. Joseph
Maude, Rector of St. Thomas, Newport, Isle of Wight,
and lost no time in entering into her husband's work.
She soon had a large class of teen-age girls in the
Sunday school, where her benign influence left its mark.

In 1847 she wrote for them this hymn, which they
learned to sing:

> Thine forever; God of love,
> Hear us from Thy throne above;
> Thine forever, may we be,
> Here and through eternity.
>
> Thine forever! Lord of life,
> Shield us through our earthly strife;
> Thou, the Life, the Truth, the Way,
> Guide us to the realms of day.
>
> Thine forever! O how blest
> They who find in Thee their rest!
> Savior, Guardian, heavenly Friend,
> O defend us to the end.
>
> Thine forever! Shepherd keep
> These, Thy frail and trembling sheep.
> Safe alone beneath Thy care,
> Let us all Thy goodness share.
>
> Thine forever! Thou our Guide,
> All our wants by Thee supplied,
> All our sins by Thee forgiven,
> Lead us, Lord, from earth to heaven.

When later on her husband was appointed to Chirk
Raubon, one of the coal districts, there was much work
to be done. Mrs. Maude soon had a large class of
colliers. Her able teaching and scholarly manner made
them regular attendants.

Then her husband died, and a new vicar was appointed. She moved back to her old home at Overton, determined to devote the rest of her life to the work she loved. Starting a class for young men, each Sunday her drawing-room was crowded. She had the gift of imparting knowledge added to a charming manner. So Mrs. Maude lived quietly on and came to the great age of ninety-four; and while bed-ridden, and awaiting the end, some men who had grown up in her Bible class asked if they might come and sing to her, her own hymn. As their voices blended together and died away, they started up an old favorite of all, "Will your anchor hold in the storms of life," and as they got to the last verse,

When our eyes behold, through the gathering night,
The city of gold, our harbor bright,
We shall anchor fast by the heavenly shore,
With the storms all past, for evermore,

came the comforting reply: "Farewell! My anchor holds!"

:-:-:-:

"THY LIFE WAS GIVEN FOR ME"

THIS IS THE first well known hymn of the gifted Frances Ridley Havergal. Her spirit, which expressed itself readily in beautiful verse, glowed with a constant fervor for the Lord. How she came to write this hymn is an interesting story.

When Miss Havergal was twenty-three, she was with her friends in Germany. She had been sight-seeing

and was tired. On coming into the house where she
was staying, a picture on the wall of her room de-
picting the sad scene of Good Friday attracted her attention. She sat down and looked at it intently. Un-
derneath were the words, "I gave My life for thee."

In a flash the words of the hymn came to her. She
wrote them down at once.

Fifteen years later, Miss Havergal, in writing to a
friend, answering a question concerning the hymn said,
"Yes, 'I gave my life for thee' is mine. And perhaps
it will interest you to know how nearly it went into
the fire instead of nearly all over the world. It was,
I think, the very first thing I wrote which could be
called a hymn, written when I was a young girl in
1859. I did not half realize what I was writing about.
I was following very far off, always doubting and fear-
ing. I scribbled the words in a few minutes on the
back of a circular, and then read them over and
thought, 'Well, this is not poetry, anyhow. I won't
trouble to write this out.' I reached out my hand to
put it in the fire, when a sudden impulse made me draw
back, and I put it, crumpled and singed, in my pocket.

"Soon after I went to see a poor old woman in the
almshouse. She began talking to me as she always
did, about her dear Savior, and I thought I would see
if she, a simple old woman, would care for these verses
which I felt sure nobody else would even care to read.

"I read them to her, and she was so delighted with
them that I copied them out in all directions, and I
have heard of their being a real blessing to many."

Thy life was given for me,
 Thy blood, O Lord, was shed
That I might ransomed be
 And quickened from the dead;
Thy life was given for me;
What have I given for Thee?

Long years were spent for me
 In weariness and woe,
That through eternity
 Thy glory I might know:
Long years were spent for me;
Have I spent one for Thee?

Thy Father's home of light,
 Thy rainbow circled throne,
Were left for earthly night,
 For wanderings sad and lone;
Yea, all was left for me;
Have I left aught for Thee?

O let my life be given,
 My years for Thee be spent;
World-fetters all be riven,
 And joy with suffering blent;
Thou gav'st Thyself for me;
I give myself to Thee.

Frances Ridley Havergal, the inspired authoress of
many beautiful hymns, died at the Mumbles, Swansea
Bay, 1879, at the early age of forty-three.

"WE PLOUGH THE FIELDS AND SCATTER"

Matthias Claudius was born near Lübeck, Holstein,
in 1740. His father was a Lutheran pastor. The boy
was educated at Jena, and lived afterwards near Ham-

burg. He was anxious to follow in his father's footsteps and become a minister, but ill health intervened. Instead he became a journalist and edited a newspaper called the *Wandesbeck Messenger.*

The year 1777 saw him the editor of a newspaper at Hesse Darmstadt. At this time he came under the influence of his friend Goethe. He became severed from his religious belief. There followed a very serious illness which seems to have been the turning-point in his career; his life became changed. He resigned his important position and returned to Wandesbeck to edit the *Messenger* in a new spirit. His means became very straitened and the fates were unkind until in 1788, the Crown Prince of Denmark presented him to a post as auditor of the Schleswig Holstein Bank at Altona.

In 1815 he retired, going to live with his daughter in Hamburg, where he died shortly afterwards, at the age of seventy-eight.

His poems were greatly regarded by his friends. Longfellow gives extracts of his work in *Poets and Poetry of Europe.*

In 1783, he wrote a sketch entitled "Paul Erdmann's Feast." It was a picture of a North German farmhouse in which was portrayed their simple, pious life. Finally, as the last load of the harvest is brought in, they sing the Peasants Song:

> *We plough the fields, and scatter*
> *The good seed on the land,*
> *But it is fed and water'd*
> *By God's almighty hand;*
> *He sends the snow in winter,*
> *The warmth to swell the grain,*
> *The breezes, and the sunshine,*

And soft refreshing rain.
All good gifts around us
Are sent from heav'n above,
Then thank the Lord, O thank the Lord,
For all His love.

He only is the Maker
Of all things near and far;
He paints the wayside flower,
He lights the evening star;
The winds and waves obey Him,
By Him the birds are fed;
Much more to us, His children,
He gives our daily bread.
All good gifts around us
Are sent from heav'n above,
Then thank the Lord, O thank the Lord,
For all His love.

We thank Thee then, O Father,
For all things bright and good,
The seed-time and the harvest,
Our life, our health, our food;
Accept the gifts we offer
For all Thy love imparts,
And what Thou most desirest,
Our humble, thankful hearts.
All good gifts around us
Are sent from heav'n above,
Then thank the Lord, O thank the Lord,
For all His love.

:-:-:-:

"WHAT A FRIEND WE HAVE IN JESUS"

JOSEPH SCRIVEN was born in Ireland, 1820, and graduated from Trinity College, Dublin. At the age of twenty-five he came to Canada and stayed at Rice

Lake, Ontario. Eventually he lived in Port Hope, Ontario, where he stayed the rest of his life. It is no secret that in 1845 life was not as easy in Canada as it is today, and Joseph's heart was very much touched by the many hardships of the poor. He lived with several families, sometimes as guest, sometimes as teacher. He had made up his mind to use his life helping others. He had his own particular way of doing so and did not escape the description, "eccentric."

Many a day he gladly gave his time to the people unable to pay. He was the friend of the poor and needy. Nothing was any trouble for those who were sick and bedridden. His clothes he gave away, until he was scanty himself. His heart was full of brotherly kindness and sympathy, but Scriven was a lonely man. The only link he had with his family at home were the slow traveling letters. In 1857, his mother was ill. She had a great sorrow. Joseph was far away, but he could write and comfort her. This he did, enclosing this inspired hymn written for her, to renew her strength and to dispel her fears:

> *What a friend we have in Jesus;*
> *All our sins and griefs to bear;*
> *What a privilege to carry*
> *Everything to God in prayer!*
> *O what peace we often forfeit,*
> *O what needless pain we bear,*
> *All because we do not carry*
> *Everything to God in prayer.*
>
> *Have we trials and temptations?*
> *Is there trouble anywhere?*
> *We should never be discouraged;*
> *Take it to the Lord in prayer.*

Can we find a friend so faithful,
Who will all our sorrows bear?
Jesus knows our every weakness,
Take it to the Lord in prayer.

Are we weak and heavy-laden,
Cumbered with a load of care?
Precious Savior, still our refuge,
Take it to the Lord in prayer.
Do thy friends despise, forsake thee?
Take it to the Lord in prayer.
In His arms He'll take and shield thee,
Thou wilt find a solace there.

Ira D. Sankey says in *My Life and Sacred Songs:*
"Mr. Scriven wrote this hymn near Port Hope, in
Canada, but its authorship remained a secret. A neighbor sitting up with him in his final illness happened
upon a manuscript copy of 'What a Friend We Have
in Jesus,' reading it with delight, and questioning
Mr. Scriven about it, he said he had composed it for
his mother to comfort her in a time of special sorrow,
not intending that anyone else should see it. Some
time later, when another neighbor asked him 'if it were
true that he had composed the hymn' his reply was,
'The Lord and I did it between us.' "

And now Joseph Scriven was a sick man. He had
fits of despondency. One sad day, in 1886, he was
found drowned near Rice Lake. No one ever knew
how it happened. His memory was much beloved in
the district. They put up a monument to the friend
of the poor. So did Joseph Scriven give Canada's
great contribution to the hymns of posterity.

:-:-:-:

Several more followed. At this
rried Mr. H. Coghill, of Coghurst
a man of substance. She was then

d the autobiography and letters

s the only one on record by this
he lived to be seventy-one and
.

"WHEN I SURVEY THE WONDROUS CROSS"

IF YOU ARE in Westminster Abbey, you may come upon the monument erected there to the memory of Isaac Watts, who was the author of this hymn. Matthew Arnold declared, "It is the finest hymn in the English language."

Watts, brought up in a Puritan home at Southampton, was once taken as a child in the arms of his mother and sat on a stone outside the prison, while she talked to his father through the bars. Freedom of religious thought had not yet been secured, and the views of the elder Watts were not those of the authorities.

As a child Watts was never strong, but his mental powers were far above the average. After some years spent as a minister at the Independent Church, Mark Lane, London, ill-health compelled him to resign. He went as a guest to the beautiful home of Sir Thomas and Lady Abdney and stayed for over thirty years, an invalid more or less all his life. His comfortable and happy surroundings there enabled him to devote his mind to many learned works. There it was that he wrote most of his beautiful hymns.

It was the age of great hymn-writers. When Watts was thirty years old, Doddridge was born. Twenty years later the two were friends. The Wesleys and Perronet, Newton and Cowper, were the inspired writers of the age.

The solemnity of this great hymn fills the heart with awe and reverence. The words are simple and direct, and are utterly sincere:

When I survey the wondrous cross
  On which the Prince of glory died,
My richest gain I count but loss,
  And pour contempt on all my pride.

Forbid it, Lord, that I should boast,
  Save in the death of Christ, my God:
All the vain things that charm me most,
  I sacrifice them to His blood.

See from His head, His hands, His feet,
  Sorrow and love flow mingled down:
Did e'er such love and sorrow meet,
  Or thorns compose so rich a crown?

Were the whole realm of nature mine,
  That were an offering far too small:
Love so amazing, so divine,
  Demands my soul, my life, my all.

The hymn owes a good deal to the tune (Rockingham) composed and adapted by Edward Miller (Mus. Bac.) 1790, forty-two years after the death of Watts.

:-:-:-:

"WORK, FOR THE NIGHT IS COMING"

When Annie Louisa Walker was a girl near teen age, she was brought out to Canada by her parents to join her two brothers who were working on the railway as engineers. They made their home in Sarnia, Ontario. Annie had a flare for writing prose and poetry. She spent all her time in these pursuits.

At twenty-three or thereabouts, she published a small book of her poems in Montreal entitled *Leaves from the Backwoods*.

Canadian Heroine.
time she met and m:
Hall, near Hastings,
about forty-seven.

Mrs. Coghill edit
of Mrs. Oliphant.

The hymn given
gifted authoress. S
died at Bath in 190

Printed in the

$ 7.95